D0615546

Due	Return	Due	Return
Date	Date	Date	

BEFORE THEIR TIME

BEFORE THEIR TIME

Six Women Writers
of the Eighteenth Century

Edited by Katharine M. Rogers

FREDERICK UNGAR PUBLISHING CO.
New York

Library of Congress Cataloging in Publication Data
Main entry under title:
Before their time.
    Includes bibliographical references.
    1. English literature—18th century. 2. English
literature—Women authors. I. Rogers, Katharine M.
PR1134.B4   810'.8'09287   78-20942
ISBN 0-8044-2742-9
ISBN 0-8044-6746-3 pbk.

CONTENTS

INTRODUCTION

The eighteenth century shows the oppression of women traditional in our culture, but it also marks the first period, in England, when they found a voice in literature. Women writers in earlier periods were exceptions—pressed by the need to express their religious experience, like Margery Kempe; or emboldened by high social position to write academic plays and translations, like Mary Herbert, Countess of Pembroke. But in the eighteenth century it was common for ladies to relate their feelings and experience in voluminous letters, and it became increasingly acceptable for them to publish and even to write for money.

Partly this was the result of improved education. Although systematic education for girls remained superficial, many people believed they should learn to write correctly and listen intelligently and be encouraged to educate themselves through solid reading. A few kindly fathers and brothers even taught girls Latin and mathematics, though most considered such subjects too difficult for them. More important, perhaps, women were participating more fully with men in social life. Especially at the Bluestocking parties in the latter part of the century, men and women met for intellectual conversation: thus women's experience was enlarged, and they were encouraged to think their minds worth developing.

At the same time, authorship was becoming more widely available as a career for women. The first professional woman

writer, Aphra Behn (1640–1689), successfully competed with
men in writing comedies for the bawdy Restoration stage. The
nature both of her work and of her private life—one affair, mul-
tiplied by gossip into total sexual looseness—made her an unsuitable example for women with a reputation to lose. But by the
middle of the century, respectable women could compete in the
literary market, though it was still considered becoming for them
to profess modesty, to claim they wrote to improve morality or
support themselves, rather than to express themselves or win
fame. Women actually dominated the field of novel-writing
toward the end of the century—one reason, no doubt, why the
novel was constantly disparaged. Of the writers represented in
this book, Anne Finch, Countess of Winchilsea, wrote to express
herself and left many of her poems unpublished. Mary Astell
published to achieve political ends, and Lady Mary Wortley
Montagu wrote for self-expression and fame, always insofar as
this was compatible with being a lady and an aristocrat: she circulated her poems in manuscript and carefully left her travel letters in the hands of one who would publish them after her death.
The last three writers in this book were professionals who could
publish without apology: Charlotte Smith and Frances Burney
wrote successful novels, while Mary Wollstonecraft was an all-
round writer as a man might be, editing and reviewing, produc-
ing political books as well as fiction.

Nevertheless, Wollstonecraft's picture of oppression in *A
Vindication of the Rights of Woman* was accurate. Whatever
progress women made in education depended on luck and their
own herculean, largely unaided efforts; they were excluded from
formal higher education and frequently told that learning was
unsuitable for them if not altogether beyond their grasp. Not
only the learned professions, but most other careers were closed
to them, so that many turned to authorship as their only resort.
And they usually made less at it than men, since novel-writing
tended to be poorly paid, and they were not rewarded, as men
often were, with a sinecure or advancement in a profession. Charlotte Smith's ceaseless labors never earned her financial security.

Women were often forced into marriage, either by family
pressure or financial need, since most had no opportunities for

supporting themselves. And marriage was oppressive. The Church preached Saint Paul's doctrine that wives should be subject to their husbands; they were to obey and please, and not to complain, no matter how they were treated. Nor, indeed, could they have resisted if they wanted to; for the law gave a husband wide power over his wife and children and complete control over the family property. Divorce was virtually impossible, and even separation discredited a wife. Of all the writers represented here, only Wollstonecraft would have openly revolted against this system; even the feminist Astell, while vigorously insisting that woman was created equal to man, agreed that she subjected herself to him in marriage. The double standard of morality that Wollstonecraft attacked in her *Vindication* was almost universally held: women had not only to be more chaste than men, but more modest and less selfish; and they were evaluated in terms of their fulfillment of men's needs, not their own.

The six writers included here represent roughly 110 years of literary expression by women, from the early poems of Winchilsea to the novels of Smith and Wollstonecraft's *Vindication*. They represent the diverse genres in which women wrote—lyric poetry, letters, journals, novels, and political tracts. Apart from the obvious fact that they were more intelligent and articulate than average, it would be difficult to generalize about them. They were all socially privileged to the extent that they had some access to education and leisure, but they ranged from upper class to lower middle (Wollstonecraft). The difficulties of rising from the lower class were, of course, even greater for women than men; Ann Yearsley, the Bristol milk-woman, is more interesting as a person than as an author.

In politics, four of these women were conservative, including the radical feminist Astell. Smith was liberal but not particularly feminist, while Wollstonecraft's radicalism led her to feminism. Three were conspicuously religious; Winchilsea's religion seems unrelated to her feminism, but Astell and Wollstonecraft grounded their claims for woman on the Christian conception that she is a rational being with an immortal soul.

Five of the women were married, three happily so, though only one was living with her husband when she did her best work. None had more than one or two children, except for Charlotte Smith, whose novels suffer artistically from the weight of her family cares and financial need. It may be significant that only one of them, Burney, had a strong and positive parental figure. Both of Winchilsea's parents died when she was a small child; Montagu, Smith, and Burney lost their mothers early, and the first two were not close to their fathers; Wollstonecraft had no cause to respect either parent. It seems likely that this lack of an emotionally compelling tie to the older generation helped these women to free themselves from restrictive convention. Burney, who adored her father, seems the least liberated of the group.

Falling in love proved to be a liberating experience for several of these women, freeing them to assert themselves. (Perhaps eighteenth-century moralists feared this when they preached that passionate love was unsuitable for women, even within marriage.) Winchilsea was supported in her writing by her loving and beloved husband, and Burney's desire to marry Alexandre d'Arblay enabled her for the first time to resist her father. Less fortunate passions seemed to have helped Montagu and Wollstonecraft to define themselves—Montagu to break off her unsatisfactory marriage, and Wollstonecraft to shape her feelings about oppression into *A Vindication of the Rights of Woman*.

Yet, although all these women were relatively liberated for their time, it would not be accurate to call them feminists. Montagu was a committed intellectual who had amused herself at twenty-one by translating Epictetus' *Enchiridion* (from a Latin version), who argued that women should be given solid education, and who remarked that "every branch" of knowledge "is entertaining." Nevertheless, she presented learning as a sort of consolation prize for women who could not make advantageous marriages. Her insistence on the happy liberty of Mohammedan Turkish women functions as a wicked comment on the Englishman's complacent assumption that England was "the paradise of wives"; but it is upsetting to note that she defined woman's liberty in terms of spending money and carrying on adulterous affairs with impunity. She had radical ideas about women, but evidently felt the need to camouflage them, just as she exhorted her granddaughter to conceal any learning she might acquire as sedulously as she would a physical defect.

On the other hand, writing is necessarily a form of self-assertion, and a woman who thinks at all will not see herself and her situation quite as a man does. Even Burney, the most conventional of the group, asserted female intelligence, simply by virtue of presenting the world through the eyes of an observant, perceptive, clearly evaluating woman. Smith, while claiming to long for a sheltered conventional life, insisted that women have a right to opinions about politics and saw that to deprive them of this right is not to keep them pure and innocent but to subject them to "mental degradation." Winchilsea was more openly unconventional, as she poured scorn on the traditional ladylike occupations and protested that writing poetry was no less suitable for women than working on decorative embroidery. Her recurrent images of liberty and imprisonment suggest a further, indirect protest against the restrictions on women.

Astell and Wollstonecraft were, of course, committed feminists. They systematically analyzed the oppression of women and campaigned to raise the condition of their whole sex. They differed on the important point of emotional freedom, for while Wollstonecraft was warmly passionate both in theory and practice, Astell firmly swept aside any claim of sexual love on the grounds that marriage was by its nature a matter of duty rather than self-fulfillment. Otherwise, their views are remarkably similar, despite their total disparity in political orientation and life style. Though Wollstonecraft was more favorable to romantic love, she no more than Astell thought it a proper basis for a lifetime relationship. Though she did not share Astell's preference for celibacy, she insisted that independence was essential for virtue and self-respect. She agreed completely that woman was not created as an adjunct to man, that her first responsibility was to develop herself as a rational virtuous being.

Both women were typical of their time in emphasizing education as the principal means to improve woman's state. Well aware of the vanity, pettiness, and other faults of contemporary women, they argued that these resulted not from female nature but from superficial and misdirected social training. Both insisted that education should be essentially the same for both sexes, since the same qualities of mind and character should be developed in women as in men. Eighteenth-century thinkers had enormous faith in the power of education, and they thought in terms of reforming individuals more than changing social institutions. The most striking difference between Astell and Wollstonecraft and modern feminists is that the former thought entirely in terms of private life. Astell disclaimed any interest in expanding career opportunities, made no mention of financial independence, and suggested no change in marriage law. Wollstonecraft, with less respect for law and more faith in marriage, did campaign to improve the legal position of wives. But one reason she attached so much importance to this reform is that she saw women primarily as wives and, above all, mothers. It is in this capacity that they contribute to society.

The attitudes of these six eighteenth-century women may seem unfamiliar because they proceed from a context of assumptions very different from our own. Yet in so many ways they speak directly to us in the twentieth century. When Astell and Winchilsea protest the idea that woman's function in life is to run a house, when Montagu exposes the absurdity of assuming incapacities in women (in "a commonwealth of rational horses . . . it would be an established maxim . . . that a mare could not be taught to pace"), when Wollstonecraft demonstrates how the ideal of sweetly dependent femininity degrades women, they are dealing with concerns of the Women's Liberation movement today.

CHRONOLOGY

	Female Authors	Male Authors
		Milton, *Paradise Lost*, 1667
		Rochester, *Satyr against Mankind*, 1675(?)
		Wycherley, *Country Wife*, 1675
		Etherege, *Man of Mode*, 1676
		Dryden, *All for Love*, 1677
		Dryden, *Absalom and Achitophel*, 1681
		Otway, *Venice Preserved*, 1682
1660 Charles II was restored to the throne	Anne Finch, Countess of Winchilsea, born, 1661	
	Mary Astell born, 1666	
	Aphra Behn, *The Rover*, 1677	
	Winchilsea began writing poems, 1680's	
1685 James II became king		
1688–89 Glorious Revolution: James II was deposed and succeeded by William and Mary	Behn, *Oroonoko*, 1688	
	Lady Mary Wortley Montagu born, 1689	
1690		

	Female Authors	Male Authors
		Dryden, *Fables*, 1700
		Congreve, *Way of the World*, 1700
		Swift, *Tale of a Tub*, 1704
		Addison and Steele, *Tatler*, 1709–11
		Addison and Steele, *Spectator*, 1711–12
		Rowe, *Jane Shore*, 1714
		Pope, *Rape of the Lock*, 1714
		Gay, Pope, Arbuthnot, *Three Hours After Marriage*, 1717
	Astell, *A Serious Proposal to the Ladies*, 1694	
1695		
1700	Astell, *Some Reflections Upon Marriage*, 1700	
1702 Anne became queen		
1705	Susannah Centlivre, *The Busy Body*, 1709	
	Mary Delariviere Manley, *The New Atalantis*, 1709	
1710	Winchilsea, *Miscellany Poems*, 1713	
1714 George I became king		
1715	Montagu wrote Turkish Letters, 1716–18	

	Female Authors	Male Authors
	Centlivre, *A Bold Stroke for a Wife*, 1718	Prior, *Poems on Several Occasions*, 1718 Defoe, *Robinson Crusoe*, 1719
1720	Winchilsea died, 1720	
1721 Walpole became first Minister		
	Jane Barker, *A Patch-Work Screen for the Ladies*, 1723	Defoe, *Moll Flanders*, 1722 Defoe, *Roxana*, 1724
1725		Swift, *Gulliver's Travels*, 1726 Thomson, *Seasons*, 1726–30
1727 George II became king	Mary Davys, *The Accomplished Rake*, 1727	Gay, *Beggar's Opera*, 1728
1730	Astell died, 1731	Pope, *Essay on Man*, 1733–34, *Moral Essay* III, *Epistle to Fortescue* (with attack on Montagu), 1733

	Female Authors	Male Authors
1735	Montagu, *The Nonsense of Common Sense*, 1737–38 Montagu lived on the continent, 1739–61	
1740		Richardson, *Pamela*, 1740 Pope, *Dunciad* (final version), 1743
1745	Sarah Fielding, *David Simple*, 1744	Richardson, *Clarissa*, 1747–48 Smollett, *Roderick Random*, 1748 Johnson, *Vanity of Human Wishes*, 1749 H. Fielding, *Tom Jones*, 1749
	Charlotte Turner Smith born, 1749	
1750		Johnson, *Rambler*, 1750–52 Gray, *Elegy Written in a Country Churchyard*, 1751 H. Fielding, *Amelia*, 1751
	Eliza Haywood, *Betsy Thoughtless*, 1751 Charlotte Lennox, *The Female Quixote*, 1752 Frances Burney d'Arblay born, 1752	
1755		Richardson, *Sir Charles Grandison*, 1753–54 Johnson, *Dictionary*, 1755
	Mary Wollstonecraft Godwin born, 1759	

	Female Authors	Male Authors
1760 George III became king		Sterne, *Tristram Shandy*, 1760–67
	Montagu died, 1762	
	Catharine Macaulay, *History of England*, 1763–83	
1765		
		Goldsmith, *Vicar of Wakefield*, 1766
		Reynolds, *Discourses*, 1769–90
	Frances Brooke, *Emily Montague*, 1769	
	Elizabeth Montagu, *Essay on the Writings and Genius of Shakespeare*, 1769	
1770		Goldsmith, *She Stoops to Conquer*, 1773
1775–83 American Revolutionary War		Burke, Speech on Conciliation with America, 1775
		Gibbon, *Decline and Fall of the Roman Empire*, 1776–88
		Sheridan, *School for Scandal*, 1777
	Burney, *Evelina*, 1778	
		Johnson, *Lives of the Poets*, 1779–81
1780		
	Burney, *Cecilia*, 1782	
		Crabbe, *The Village*, 1783

	Female Authors	Male Authors
1785		Cowper, *The Task*, 1785
	Hester Thrale Piozzi, *Anecdotes of the Late Samuel Johnson*, 1786	Burns, *Poems, Chiefly in the Scottish Dialect*, 1786
	Elizabeth Inchbald, *Such Things Are*, 1787	
	Smith, *Emmeline*, 1788	
	Wollstonecraft, *Mary: A Fiction*, 1788	
1789 French Revolution began		
1790	Wollstonecraft, *Vindication of the Rights of Men*, 1790	Burke, *Reflections on the Revolution in France*, 1790
	Inchbald, *A Simple Story*, 1791	Paine, *The Rights of Man*, 1791
		Boswell, *Life of Johnson*, 1791
	Hannah More, *Village Politics*, 1792	
	Wollstonecraft, *Vindication of the Rights of Woman*, 1792	
	Smith, *Desmond*, 1792	
	Smith, *The Old Manor House*, 1793	Godwin, *Political Justice*, 1793
	Smith, *The Banished Man*, 1794	Blake, *Songs of Experience*, 1794
	Ann Radcliffe, *The Mysteries of Udolpho*, 1794	

	Female Authors	Male Authors
1795	Maria Edgeworth, *Letters to Literary Ladies*, 1795 Burney, *Camilla*, 1796 Wollstonecraft died, 1797 Radcliffe, *The Italian*, 1797	Wordsworth and Coleridge, *Lyrical Ballads*, 1798
1800	Edgeworth, *Castle Rackrent*, 1800 Smith died, 1806 More, *Coelebs in Search of a Wife*, 1809	
1810	Jane Austen, *Sense and Sensibility*, 1811 Burney, *The Wanderer*, 1814	
1820 George III died	Burney died, 1840	

ANNE FINCH,
COUNTESS OF WINCHILSEA

Anne Finch, Countess of Winchilsea (1661–1720), was fortunate in her social position, her loving and appreciative husband, and the political chance which early sent them out of public life. Heneage Finch met and fell in love with Anne Kingsmill at Court, where they were attendants upon James, Duke of York (later James II) and his wife Mary of Modena. When James was deposed, they retired to the country seat of the Earl of Winchilsea (Heneage Finch later succeeded to the title), where he devoted himself to study and she to poetry and enjoyment of nature. In other circumstances she might well have lacked the leisure and encouragement necessary to nurture her poetic gift. Even so, despite the support of husband and friends, she constantly felt the need to justify the use of her talent.

Winchilsea used the genres of her period—love lyrics, satires, fables, meditative nature pieces—and her poems show typical Augustan reticence and concern for form. Yet as a woman she expressed Augustan attitudes with a difference: her love lyrics are more idealistic and more personally felt, and she is remarkably free of the Augustan tendency to make public pronouncements. It is interesting to contrast her poems to her husband with Matthew Prior's to Chloe, and "A Nocturnal Reverie" with Alexander Pope's "Windsor Forest."

Though women could not participate fully in the intellectual life of her day, Winchilsea was acquainted with leading con-

1

temporary writers such as Pope and Jonathan Swift, who had mixed feelings about her. She published a volume of poems in 1713, but left many more, including the more personal and feminist ones, in a beautiful manuscript copy, presumably hoping that they would be published after her death. (They did not appear until 1903.) Her "Introduction" opened this collection. The biblical precedents she cites here may seem irrelevant today, but were called for in an age when the Bible was constantly cited to prove woman's inferiority.

THE INTRODUCTION

Did I, my lines intend for public view,
How many censures would their faults pursue,
Some would, because such words they do affect,
Cry they're insipid, empty, uncorrect.
And many have attained, dull and untaught,
The name of wit, only by finding fault.
True judges might condemn their want of wit,
And all might say, they're by a woman writ.
Alas! a woman that attempts the pen,
Such an intruder on the rights of men,   10
Such a presumptuous creature is esteemed,
The fault can by no virtue be redeemed.
They tell us, we mistake our sex and way;
Good breeding, fashion, dancing, dressing, play
Are the accomplishments we should desire;
To write, or read, or think, or to enquire
Would cloud our beauty, and exhaust our time,
And interrupt the conquests of our prime;
Whilst the dull manage of a servile house
Is held by some our utmost art, and use.   20
       Sure 'twas not ever thus, nor are we told
Fables, of women that excelled of old;
To whom, by the diffusive hand of Heaven
Some share of wit and poetry was given.
On that glad day, on which the Ark returned,
The holy pledge, for which the land had mourned,
The joyful tribes attend it on the way,
The Levites do the sacred charge convey,
Whilst various instruments before it play;
Here, holy virgins in the concert join,   30
The louder notes to soften and refine,
And with alternate verse, complete the hymn divine.
Lo! the young poet, after God's own heart,
By Him inspired, and taught the Muses' art,
Returned from conquest, a bright chorus meets,
That sing his slain ten thousand in the streets.

In such loud numbers they his acts declare,
Proclaim the wonders of his early war,
That Saul upon the vast applause does frown,
And feels its mighty thunder shake the crown.   40
What, can the threatened judgment now prolong?
Half of the kingdom is already gone;
The fairest half, whose influence guides the rest,
Have David's empire o'er their hearts confessed.
     A woman here leads fainting Israel on,
She fights, she wins, she triumphs with a song,
Devout, majestic, for the subject fit,
And far above her arms exalts her wit,
Then, to the peaceful, shady palm withdraws,
And rules the rescued nation with her laws.   50
How are we fallen, fallen by mistaken rules?
And Education's, more than Nature's fools,
Debarred from all improvements of the mind,
And to be dull, expected and designed;
And if some one would soar above the rest,
With warmer fancy, and ambition pressed,
So strong, th'opposing faction still appears,
The hopes to thrive can ne'er outweigh the fears,
Be cautioned then my Muse, and still retired;
Nor be despised, aiming to be admired;   60
Conscious of wants, still with contracted wing,
To some few friends, and to thy sorrows sing;
For groves of laurel thou wert never meant;
Be dark enough thy shades, and be thou there content.

THE LOSS

She sighed, but soon it mixed with common air,
Too fleet a witness for her deep despair;
She wept, but tears no lasting grief can show,
For tears will fail and ebb, as well as flow.
She would her tongue to the sad subject force,
But all great passions are above discourse.

Thy heart alone, Ardelia, with it trust,
There grave it deep, alas! 'twill fall to dust.
Urania is no more, to me no more,
All these combined, can ne'er that loss deplore.

THE CONSOLATION

See, Phoebus breaking from the willing skies,
See, how the soaring lark does with him rise,
And through the air, is such a journey borne
As if she never thought of a return.
Now, to his noon, behold him proudly go,
And look with scorn, on all that's great below.
A Monarch he, and ruler of the day,
A favorite She, that in his beams does play.
Glorious, and high, but shall they ever be,
Glorious, and high, and fixed where now we see?
No, both must fall, nor can their stations keep,
She to the earth, and he below the deep,
At night both fall, but the swift hand of time
Renews the morning, and again they climb,
Then let no cloudy change create my sorrow,
I'll think 'tis night, and I may rise tomorrow.

A LETTER TO DAPHNIS, APRIL 2, 1685

This to the crown and blessing of my life,
The much loved husband of a happy wife.
To him whose constant passion found the art
To win a stubborn and ungrateful heart;
And to the world by tenderest proof discovers
They err, who say that husbands can't be lovers.
With such return of passion, as is due,
Daphnis I love, Daphnis my thoughts pursue,
Daphnis, my hopes, my joys, are bounded all in you:
Even I, for Daphnis, and my promise sake,

What I in women censure, undertake.
But this from love, not vanity, proceeds;
You know who writes; and I who 'tis that reads.
Judge not my passion by my want of skill,
Many love well, though they express it ill;
And I your censure could with pleasure bear,
Would you but soon return, and speak it here.

TO MR. F. NOW EARL OF W.

Who going abroad, had desired Ardelia to write some verses
upon whatever subject she thought fit, against his return in
the evening   *Written in the Year 1689*

No sooner, Flavio, was you gone,
But, your injunction thought upon,
    Ardelia took the pen;
Designing to perform the task,
Her Flavio did so kindly ask,
    Ere he returned again.

Unto Parnassus straight she sent,
And bid the messenger that went
    Unto the Muses' Court,
Assure them, she their aid did need,   10
And begged they'd use their utmost speed,
    Because the time was short.

The hasty summons was allowed;
And being well-bred, they rose and bowed,
    And said, they'd post away;
That well they did Ardelia know,
And that no female's voice below
    They sooner would obey:

That many of that rhyming train,
On like occasions, sought in vain   20
    Their industry t'excite;

But for Ardelia all they'd leave:
Thus flattering can the Muse deceive,
    And wheedle us to write.

Yet, since there was such haste required;
To know the subject 'twas desired,
    On which they must infuse;
That they might temper words and rules,
And with their counsel carry tools,
    As country-doctors use.   30

Wherefore to cut off all delays,
'Twas soon replied, a husband's praise
    (Though in these looser times)
Ardelia gladly would rehearse
A husband's, who indulged her verse,
    And now required her rhymes.

A husband! echoed all around:
And to Parnassus sure that sound
    Had never yet been sent;
Amazement in each face was read,   40
In haste th'affrighted sisters fled,
    And unto Council went.

Erato cried, since Grisel's days,
Since *Troy-Town* pleased, and *Chevy Chase*,
    No such design was known;
And 'twas their business to take care,
It reached not to the public ear,
    Or got about the Town:

Nor came where evening *beaux* were met
O'er *billet-doux* and chocolate,   50
    Lest it destroyed the House:
For in that place, who could dispense
(That wore his clothes with common sense)
    With mention of a spouse?

'Twas put unto the vote at last,
And in the negative it passed,
    None to her aid should move;
Yet since Ardelia was a friend,
Excuses 'twas agreed to send,
    Which plausible might prove   60

That Pegasus of late had been
So often rid through thick and thin,
    With neither fear nor wit;
In panegyric been so spurred,
He could not from the stall be stirred,
    Nor would endure the bit.

Melpomene had given a bond,
By the new House alone to stand,
    And write of war and strife;
Thalia, she had taken fees,   70
And stipends from the Patentees,
    And durst not for her life.

Urania only liked the choice;
Yet not to thwart the public voice,
    She whispering did impart:
They need no foreign aid invoke,
Nor help to draw a moving stroke,
    Who dictate from the heart.

Enough! the pleased Ardelia cried;
And slighting every Muse beside,   80
    Consulting now her breast,
Perceived that every tender thought,
Which from abroad she'd vainly sought,
    Did there in silence rest:

And should unmoved that post maintain,
Till in his quick return again,
    Met in some neighboring grove,

(Where Vice nor Vanity appear)
Her Flavio them alone might hear,
    In all the sounds of love. 90

For since the world does so despise
Hymen's endearments and its ties,
    They should mysterious be;
Till we that pleasure too possess
(Which makes their fancied happiness)
    Of stolen secrecy.

ARDELIA'S ANSWER TO EPHELIA

    who had invited her to come to her in town—reflecting on
    the coquetry and detracting humour of the age

Me, dear Ephelia, me, in vain you court
With all your powerful influence, to resort
To that great Town, where friendship can but have
The few spare hours, which meaner pleasures leave.
No! Let some shade, or your large palace be
Our place of meeting, love, and liberty;
To thoughts, and words, and all endearments free.
But, to those walls, excuse my slow repair;
Who have no business, or diversion there;
No dazzling beauty, to attract the gaze 10
Of wondering crowds to my applauded face;
Nor to my little wit, th'ill nature joined,
To pass a general censure on mankind:
To call the young and unaffected, fools;
Dull all the grave, that live by moral rules;
To say the soldier brags, who, asked, declares
The nice escapes and dangers of his wars,
The poet's vain, that knows his unmatched worth,
And dares maintain what the best Muse brings forth:
Yet, this the humour of the age is grown, 20
And only conversation of the Town.

In satire versed, and sharp detraction, be,
And you're accomplished for all company.

II

     When my last visit, I to London made,
Me, to Almeria, wretched chance betrayed;
The fair Almeria, in this art so known,
That she discerns all failings, but her own.
With a loud welcome, and a strict embrace,
Kisses on kisses, in a public place,
Sh'extorts a promise, that next day I dine   30
With her, who for my sight, did hourly pine;
And wonders, how so far I can remove,
From the *beau monde*, and the dull country love;
Yet vows, if but an afternoon 'twould cost
To see me there, she could resolve almost
To quit the Town, and for that time, be lost.
     My word I keep, we dine, then rising late,
Take coach, which long had waited at the gate.
About the streets, a tedious ramble go,
To see this monster, or that wax work show,   40
Or any thing, that may the time bestow.
When by a church we pass, I ask to stay,
Go in, and my devotions humbly pay
To that great Power, whom all the wise obey.
Whilst the gay thing, light as her feathered dress,
Flies round the coach, and does each cushion press,
Through every glass, her several graces shows,
This, does her face, and that, her shape expose,
To envying beauties and admiring beaux.
One stops, and as expected, all extolls,   50
Clings to the door, and on his elbow lolls,
Thrusts in his head, at once to view the fair,
And keep his curls from discomposing air,
Then thus proceeds—
                         My wonder it is grown
To find Almeria here, and here alone.

Where are the nymphs, that round you used to crowd,
Of your long courted approbation proud,
Learning from you, how to erect their hair,
And in perfection, all their habit wear,
To place a patch, in some peculiar way,   60
That may an unmarked smile, to sight betray,
And the vast genius of the sex, display?
     Pity me then (she cries) and learn the fate
That makes me porter to a temple gate;
Ardelia came to Town, some weeks ago,
Who does on books her rural hours bestow,
And is so rustic in her clothes and mien,
'Tis with her ungenteel but to be seen,
Did not a long acquaintance plead excuse;
Besides, she likes no wit that's now in use,   70
Despises courtly vice, and plainly says,
That sense and nature should be found in plays,
And therefore, none will e'er be brought to see
But those of Dryden, Etherege, or Lee,
And some few authors, old, and dull to me.
To her I did engage my coach and day,
And here must wait, while she within does pray.
Ere twelve was struck, she calls me from my bed,
Nor once observes how well my toilet's spread;
Then, drinks the fragrant tea contented up,   80
Without a compliment upon the cup,
Though to the ships, for the first choice I steered,
Through such a storm, as the stout bargemen feared;
Lest that a praise, which I have long engrossed
Of the best china equipage, be lost.
Of fashions now, and colours I discoursed,
Detected shops that would expose the worst,
What silks, what lace, what ribbons she must have,
And by my own, an ample pattern gave;
To which, she cold and unconcerned replied,   90
I deal with one that does all these provide,
Having of other cares, enough beside;
And in a cheap, or an ill chosen gown,

Can value blood that's nobler than my own,
And therefore hope, myself not to be weighed
By gold, or silver, on my garments laid;
Or that my wit or judgment should be read
In an uncommon colour on my head.

    Stupid! and dull, the shrugging zany cries;
When, service ended, me he moving spies,   100
Hastes to conduct me out, and in my ear
Drops some vile praise, too low for her to hear;
Which to avoid, more than the begging throng,
I reach the coach, that swiftly rolls along,
Lest to Hyde Park, we should too late be brought,
And lose ere night, an hour of finding fault.
Arrived, she cries,—

               That awkward creature see,
A fortune born, and would a beauty be
Could others but believe, as fast as she.
Round me I look, some monster to descry,   110
Whose wealthy acres must a title buy,
Support my Lord, and be, since his have failed,
With the high shoulder, on his race entailed;
When to my sight, a lovely face appears,
Perfect in everything, but growing years;
This I defend, to do my judgment right,
Can you dispraise a skin so smooth, so white,
That blush, which o'er such well turned cheeks does rise,
That look of youth, and those enlivened eyes?
She soon replies,—

             That skin, which you admire,   120
Is shrunk, and sickly, could you view it nigher.
The crimson lining and uncertain light,
Reflects that blush, and paints her to the sight.
Trust me, the look, which you commend, betrays
A want of sense, more than the want of days,
And those wild eyes, that round the circle stray,
Seem as her wits had but mistook their way.
As I did mine, I to myself repeat,
When by this envious side I took my seat:

Oh! for my groves, my country walks, and bowers,   130
Trees blast not trees, nor flowers envenom flowers,
As beauty here, all beauty's praise devours.
But noble Piso passes,—
                        He's a wit.
As some (she says) would have it, though as yet
No line he in a lady's fan has writ,
Ne'er on their dress, in verse, soft things would say,
Or with loud clamour overpowered a play,
And right or wrong, prevented the third day;
To read in public places, is not known,
Or in his chariot, here appears alone;   140
Bestows no hasty praise on all that's new.
When first this coach came out to public view,
Met in a visit, he presents his hand
And takes me out, I make a willful stand,
Expecting, sure, this would applause invite,
And often turned that way, to guide his sight;
Till finding him wrapped in a silent thought,
I asked, if that the painter well had wrought,
Who then replied, he has in the fable erred,
Covering Adonis with a monstrous beard;   150
Made Hercules (who by his club is shown)
A gentler fop than any of the Town,
Whilst Venus, from a bog is rising seen,
And eyes asquint are given to beauty's queen.
I had no patience, longer to attend,
And know 'tis want of wit, to discommend.
   Must Piso then! be judged by such as these,
Piso, who from the Latin, Virgil frees,
Who loosed the bands, which old Silenus bound,
And made our Albion rocks repeat the mystic sound,   160
"Whilst all he sung was present to our eyes
And as he rais'd his verse, the poplars seemed to rise"?
Scarce could I in my breast my thoughts contain,
Or for this folly, hide my just disdain.
When see, she says, observe my best of friends,
And through the window, half her length extends

Exalts her voice, that all the ring may hear;
How fulsomely she oft repeats my dear,
Lets fall some doubtful words, that we may know
There still a secret is, betwixt them two,   170
And makes a sign, the small white hand to show.
When, Fate be praised, the coachman slacks the reins,
And o'er my lap, no longer now she leans,
But how her choice I like, does soon enquire?
     Can I dislike, I cry, what all admire,
Discreet, and witty, civil and refined,
Nor in her person fairer than her mind,
Is young Alinda, if report be just;
For half the character, my eyes I trust.
What, changed, Almeria, on a sudden cold,   180
As if I of your friend some tale had told?
No, she replies, but when I hear her praise,
A secret failing does my pity raise,
Damon she loves, and 'tis my daily care,
To keep the passion from the public ear,
I ask, amazed, if this she has revealed,
No, but 'tis true, she cries, though much concealed;
I have observed it long, nor would betray
But to yourself, what now with grief I say,
Who this, to none but confidants must break,   190
Nor they to others, but in whispers, speak;
I am her friend and must consult her fame.
More was she saying, when fresh objects came,
Now what's that thing, she cries, Ardelia, guess?
A woman sure.—
                Ay, and a poetess,
They say she writes, and 'tis a common jest.
Then sure sh'has publicly the skill professed,
I soon reply, or makes that gift her pride,
And all the world, but scribblers, does deride;
Sets out lampoons, where only spite is seen,   200
Not filled with female wit, but female spleen.
Her flourished name does o'er a song expose,
Which through all ranks, down to the carman, goes.

Or poetry is on her picture found,
In which she sits, with painted laurel crowned.
If no such flies, no vanity defile
The Heliconian balm, the sacred oil,
Why should we from that pleasing art be tied,
Or like state prisoners, pen and ink denied?
But see, the sun his chariot home has driven   210
From the vast shining ring of spacious Heaven,
Nor after him celestial beauties stay,
But crowd with sparkling wheels the milky way.
Shall we not then, the great example take
And ours below, with equal speed forsake?
When to your favours, adding this one more,
You'll stop, and leave me thankful, at my door.
How! ere you've in the Drawing-room appeared,
And all the follies there beheld and heard.
Since you've been absent, such intrigues are grown;   220
Such new coquets and fops are to be shown,
Without their sight you must not leave the Town.
Excuse me, I reply, my eyes ne'er feast
Upon a fool, though ne'er so nicely dressed.
Nor is it music to my burthened ear
The unripe pratings of our sex to hear,
A noisy girl, who has at fifteen talked more
Than grandmother or mother heretofore,
In all the cautious, prudent years they bore.
Statesmen there are (she cries), whom I can show   230
That bear the kingdom's cares, on a bent brow;
Who take the weight of politics by grains,
And to the least, know what each skull contains,
Who's to be coached, who talked to when abroad,
Who but the smile must have, and who the nod;
And when this is the utmost of their skill,
'Tis not much wonder, if affairs go ill.
Then for the churchmen—
                              Hold, my lodging's here;
Nor can I longer a reproof forbear
When sacred things nor persons she would spare.   240

We parted thus, the night in peace I spent,
And the next day, with haste and pleasure went
To the best seat of famed and fertile Kent.
Where let me live from all detraction free
Till thus the world is criticized by me;
Till friend, and foe, I treat with such despite
May I no scorn, the worst of ills, excite.

THE BIRD AND THE ARRAS

By near resemblance see that bird betrayed
Who takes the well wrought arras for a shade
There hopes to perch and with a cheerful tune
O'er-pass the scorchings of the sultry noon.
But soon repulsed by the obdurate scene
How swift she turns, but turns alas in vain.
That piece a grove, this shows an ambient sky
Where imitated fowl their pinions ply,
Seeming to mount in flight and aiming still more high.
All she outstrips and with a moment's pride
Their understation silent does deride
Till the dashed ceiling strikes her to the ground,
No intercepting shrub to break the fall is found.
Recovering breath the window next she gains
Nor fears a stop from the transparent panes.

                    . . . .

But we digress and leave th'imprisoned wretch
Now sinking low, now on a loftier stretch
Fluttering in endless circles of dismay
Till some kind hand directs the certain way
Which through the casement an escape affords
And leads to ample space, the only Heaven of birds.

A SONG

'Tis strange, this heart within my breast,
    Reason opposing, and her powers,
Cannot one gentle moment rest,
    Unless it knows what's done in yours.

In vain I ask it of your eyes,
    Which subtly would my fears control;
For Art has taught them to disguise,
    Which Nature made t'explain the soul.

In vain that sound, your voice affords,
    Flatters sometimes my easy mind;
But of too vast extent are words
    In them the jewel truth to find.

Then let my fond enquiries cease,
    And so let all my troubles end:
For, sure, that heart shall ne'er know peace,
    Which on another's does depend.

A SONG

The nymph, in vain, bestows her pains,
That seeks to thrive, where Bacchus reigns;
In vain, are charms, or smiles, or frowns,
All images his torrent drowns.

Flames to the head he may impart,
But makes an island, of the heart;
So inaccessible, and cold,
That to be his, is to be old.

THE UNEQUAL FETTERS

Could we stop the time that's flying
    Or recall it when 'tis past
Put far off the day of dying
    Or make youth for ever last
To love would then be worth our cost.

But since we must lose those graces
    Which at first your hearts have won
And you seek for in new faces
    When our spring of life is done
It would but urge our ruin on.

Free as Nature's first intention
    Was to make us, I'll be found
Nor by subtle Man's invention
    Yield to be in fetters bound
By one that walks a freer round.

Marriage does but slightly tie men
    Whilst close prisoners we remain
They the larger slaves of Hymen
    Still are begging love again
At the full length of all their chain.

THE YOUNG RAT AND HIS DAM,
THE COCK AND THE CAT

No cautions of a matron, old and sage,
Young Rattlehead to prudence could engage;
But forth the offspring of her bed would go,
Nor reason gave, but that he *would* do so.
Much counsel was, at parting, thrown away,
Even all, that Mother-Rat to Son could say;
Who followed him with utmost reach of sight,
Then, lost in tears, and in abandoned plight,

Turned to her mournful cell, and bid the world Good Night.
But Fortune, kinder than her boding thought,   10
In little time the vagrant homewards brought,
Raised in his mind, and mended in his dress,
Who the *bel-air* did every way confess,
Had learnt to flour his wig, nor brushed away
The falling meal, that on his shoulders lay;
And from a nutshell, wimbled by a worm,
Took snuff, and could the government reform.
The mother, weeping from maternal love,
To see him thus prodigiously improve,
Expected mighty changes too, within,   20
And wisdom to avoid the cat and gin.
Whom did you chiefly note, Sweetheart, quoth she,
Of all the strangers you abroad did see?
Who graced you most, or did your fancy take?
The younger rat then cursed a noisy rake,
That barred the best acquaintance he could make;
And feared him so, he trembled every part;
Nor to describe him, scarce could have the heart.
High on his feet (quoth he) himself he bore,
And terribly, in his own language, swore;   30
A feathered arm came out from either side,
Which loud he clapped, and combatants defied,
And to each leg a bayonet was tied:
And certainly his head with wounds was sore;
For that, and both his cheeks a sanguine colour wore.
Near him there lay the creature I admired,
And for a friend by sympathy desired:
His make, like ours, as far as tail and feet,
With coat of fur in parallel do meet;
Yet seeming of a more exalted race,   40
Though humble meekness beautified his face:
A purring sound composed his gentle mind,
Whilst frequent slumbers did his eyelids bind;
Whose soft, contracted paw lay calmly still,
As if unused to prejudice, or kill.
I paused a while, to meditate a speech,

And now was stepping just within his reach;
When that rude clown began his hectoring cry,
And made me for my life, and from th'attempt to fly.
Indeed 'twas time, the shivering beldam said,   50
To scour the plain, and be of life afraid.
Thou base, degenerate seed of injured rats,
Thou veriest fool (she cried) of all my brats;
Wouldst thou have shaken hands with hostile cats,
And dost not yet thine own, and country's foe,
At this expence of time and travel know?
Alas! that swearing, staring, bullying thing,
That tore his throat, and blustered with his wing,
Was but some paltry, dunghill, craven cock,
Who serves the early household for a clock.   60
And we his oats and barley often steal,
Nor fear, he should revenge the pilfered meal;
Whilst that demure, and seeming harmless puss
Herself and mewing chits regales with us.
If then, of useful sense thou'st gained no more,
Than ere thou'dst past the threshold of my door;
Be here, my son, content to dress and dine,
Steeping the list of beauties in thy wine,
And neighboring vermin with false gloss outshine.
    Amongst mankind a thousand fops we see,   70
Who in their rambles learn no more than thee;
Cross o'er the Alps, and make the Tour of France
To learn a paltry song or antic dance;
Bringing their noddles and valises packed
With mysteries, from shops and tailors wrecked:
But what may prejudice their native land,
Whose troops are raising, or whose fleet is manned,
Ne'er moves their thoughts, nor do they understand.
Thou, my dear Rattlehead, and such as these
Might keep at home, and brood on sloth and ease;   80
Whilst others, more adapted to the age,
May vigorously in warlike feats engage,
And live on foreign spoils, or dying thin the stage.

TO THE NIGHTINGALE

Exert thy voice, sweet harbinger of spring!
    This moment is thy time to sing,
    This moment I attend to praise,
And set my numbers to thy lays.
    Free as thine shall be my song;
    As thy music, short, or long.
Poets, wild as thee, were born,
    Pleasing best when unconfined,
    When to please is least designed,
Soothing but their cares to rest;   10
    Cares do still their thoughts molest,
    And still th'unhappy poet's breast,
Like thine, when best he sings, is placed against a thorn.
She begins, Let all be still!
    Muse, thy promise now fulfill!
Sweet, oh! sweet, still sweeter yet
Can thy words such accents fit,
Canst thou syllables refine,
Melt a sense that shall retain
Still some spirit of the brain,   20
Till with sounds like these it join.
    'Twill not be! then change thy note;
    Let division shake thy throat.
Hark! Division now she tries;
Yet as far the Muse outflies.
    Cease then, prithee, cease thy tune;
    Trifler, wilt thou sing till June?
Till thy business all lies waste,
And the time of building's past!
    Thus we poets that have speech,   30
Unlike what thy forests teach,
    If a fluent vein be shown
    That's transcendent to our own,
Criticize, reform, or preach,
Or censure what we cannot reach.

A NOCTURNAL REVERIE

In such a night, when every louder wind
Is to its distant cavern safe confined;
And only gentle Zephyr fans his wings,
And lonely Philomel, still waking, sings;
Or from some tree, famed for the owl's delight,
She, hollowing clear, directs the wanderer right:
In such a night, when passing clouds give place,
Or thinly veil the heavens' mysterious face;
When in some river, overhung with green,
The waving moon and trembling leaves are seen;   10
When freshened grass now bears itself upright,
And makes cool banks to pleasing rest invite,
Whence springs the woodbind, and the bramble-rose,
And where the sleepy cowslip sheltered grows;
Whilst now a paler hue the foxglove takes,
Yet checkers still with red the dusky brakes;
When scattered glow-worms, but in twilight fine,
Show trivial beauties watch their hour to shine;
Whilst Salisbury stands the test of every light,
In perfect charm and perfect virtue bright: 20
When odours, which declined repelling day,
Through temperate air uninterrupted stray;
When darkened groves their softest shadows wear,
And falling waters we distinctly hear;
When through the gloom more venerable shows
Some ancient fabric, awful in repose,
While sunburnt hills their swarthy looks conceal,
And swelling haycocks thicken up the vale:
When the loosed horse now, as his pasture leads,
Comes slowly grazing through th'adjoining meads.   30
Whose stealing pace, and lengthened shade we fear,
Till torn up forage in his teeth we hear:
When nibbling sheep at large pursue their food,
And unmolested kine rechew the cud;
When curlews cry beneath the village-walls,
And to her straggling brood the partridge calls;

Their shortlived jubilee the creatures keep,
Which but endures, whilst tyrant-man does sleep;
When a sedate content the spirit feels,
And no fierce light disturbs, whilst it reveals;   40
But silent musings urge the mind to seek
Something, too high for syllables to speak;
Till the free soul to a composedness charmed,
Finding the elements of rage disarmed,
O'er all below a solemn quiet grown,
Joys in th'inferiour world, and thinks it like her own:
In such a night let me abroad remain,
Till morning breaks, and all's confused again;
Our cares, our toils, our clamours are renewed,
Or pleasures, seldom reached, again pursued.   50

Notes

THE INTRODUCTION
Lines 25–50 refer to three episodes in the Old Testament: 1) the Israel-
ites sang and played instruments to celebrate bringing the Ark of the
Covenant into Jerusalem (*I Chronicles*, chapter 15. The "holy virgins,"
however, seem to be Winchilsea's addition); 2) the women of Israel,
greeting the victorious David with songs, praised his achievement over
King Saul's (*I Samuel*, chapter 18); 3) the judge Deborah led the Israel-
ites to victory and then composed a triumphant song (*Judges*, chapters
4 and 5).

TO MR. F. NOW EARL OF W.
Stanza 8. Erato is the Muse of love poetry. Grisel or Griselda was the
model of a patient devoted wife, celebrated in medieval literature.
"Troy-Town," referring to Homer's *Iliad* or possibly John Lydgate's
Troy-book (1412–20), and the old ballad "Chevy Chase" (fifteenth
century) are examples of literature hopelessly out of fashion.
Stanza 9. "dispense with"—excuse
Stanza 11. Pegasus has been overworked in the composition of poetical
tributes to William, the new king *(Reynolds).*

Stanza 12. Melpomene, the Muse of tragedy, and Thalia, the Muse of comedy, are committed to inspiring only work for the one licensed theatre ("House") in London, whose managers held a patent from the government.

Stanza 13. Urania is the Muse of heavenly love.

ARDELIA'S ANSWER TO EPHELIA

Line 75. At this point the following lines were added in the margin of the manuscript:

> Even Wycherley admires whose biting pen
> Reveals our frailty to insulting men,
> And speaks of Otway with such delight
> As if no other pen could move or write.   *(Reynolds)*

William Wycherley satirized just such women as Almeria; Ardelia's ability to appreciate him shows her superiority to the failings conventionally charged to women.

Line 105. Fashionable people drove their coaches around a circular drive in Hyde Park ("the circle," *line 126;* "the ring," *line 167*) to see and be seen.

Line 133. Piso is Wentworth Dillon, Earl of Roscommon (1633?–1685), who wrote a blank verse translation of Horace's "Ars Poetica" (1680) and an "Essay on Translated Verse" (1684).

Line 138. Since the playwright was paid by the net profits of the third night his play was performed, to prevent its running this long would deprive him of the reward for his work.

Line 218. Fashionable people regularly gathered at the Drawing-room, a public reception at Court.

Bibliographical Note

The only complete edition of Winchilsea's poems is that of Myra Reynolds, *The Poems of Anne Countess of Winchilsea* (Chicago: University of Chicago Press, 1903), which is out of print. Katharine Rogers has edited a selection of her poems (New York: Frederick Ungar, 1978).

Very little has been published about Winchilsea. William Wordsworth drew attention to her as a nature poet in his "Essay Supplementary to the Preface" (1815). Reuben A. Brower—in "Lady Winchilsea and the Poetic Tradition of the Seventeenth Century," *Studies in*

Philology, XLII (1945), 61–80—argued convincingly that her poetry is not preromantic, but characteristic of its period. Katharine Rogers discussed Winchilsea specifically as a woman poet in "Anne Finch, Countess of Winchilsea—An Augustan Woman Poet," in *Shakespeare's Sisters,* edited by Sandra Gilbert and Susan Gubar (Bloomington: Indiana University Press, 1979).

MARY ASTELL

Little is known of what influences formed Mary Astell (1666–1731), how she got her education (tradition says a clergyman uncle taught her Latin), and how she established herself financially and socially so as to lead a successful independent life. She came from a middle-class provincial family and at the age of twenty moved from Newcastle to Chelsea, where she became a good friend of several upper-class women, including Lady Mary Wortley Montagu, a less unconventional feminist. Astell was forbidding in appearance, blunt in manners, and utterly contemptuous of masculine gallantry, which she regarded "as insults in disguise, impertinently offered by men through a secret persuasion that all women were fools."

Astell had a distinguished career in controversial writing, ranging from scholarly works like *Letters Concerning the Love of God* to polemical ones such as *A Fair Way with the Dissenters,* but always defending the established order in Church and State. All her tracts show professional skill, vigor, and knowledge of the issues. Many clergymen respected her intellect and valued her contributions in defense of the Church of England, though one deplored her tendency to be "now and then a little offensive and shocking in her expressions, which I wonder at, because a civil turn of words . . . is what her sex is always mistress of."

Her strong conservatism did not, however, inhibit her from radical thinking about the position of her sex. This produced *A*

Serious Proposal to the Ladies (1694), a project for establishing a "monastery" or "religious retirement" for women, and *Some Reflections upon Marriage Occasioned by the Duke and Duchess of Mazarine's Case* (1700), inspired by the Duchess's apologia for eloping from her insane husband. Both books were popular enough to go through several editions. The *Proposal* attracted considerable attention, much of it respectful, but met the fate Astell feared: no one was sufficiently persuaded to put its principles into practice. The religious retirement reminded people too much of a Roman Catholic convent, and even feminist sympathizers thought the dangers of popery outweighed the interests of women.

The institution Astell proposed did indeed resemble an enlightened convent, except that there were no permanent vows and its explicit aim was self-development. The women would divide their time among prayer, study, teaching, and good works; they would develop their minds through substantial reading and intellectual conversation. However, Astell does not suggest either practical application or external recognition; indeed, she explicitly disclaims any desire to expand women's opportunities for careers and apparently assumes they will be supported by their families.

Her unwillingness to challenge established law, together with her own preference for celibacy, accounts for the relative indifference to improving the lot of wives which we see in *Some Reflections on Marriage*. While clearly recognizing their oppression, she does not suggest that the laws of state or church be modified to alleviate it. Perhaps, however, the irony which pervades much of this tract was meant to extend to its apparently uncompromising insistence on the subjection of wives.

A SERIOUS PROPOSAL TO THE LADIES

Astell opens her *Proposal* by declaring that her aim is to awaken women to their real interest by convincing them to value themselves not on "the pitiful conquest of some worthless heart," but on the genuinely valuable qualities of mind and character which will earn them the esteem of good men and the approbation of God:

Women need not take up with mean things, since (if they are not wanting to themselves) they are capable of the best. Neither God nor Nature have excluded them from being ornaments to their families, and useful in their generation; there is therefore no reason they should be content to be ciphers in the world, useless at the best, and in a little time a burden and nuisance to all about them. And 'tis very great pity that they who are so apt to over-rate themselves in smaller matters, should, where it most concerns them to know, and stand upon their value, be so insensible of their own worth.

The cause therefore of the defects we labour under is, if not wholly, yet at least in the first place, to be ascribed to the mistakes of our education, which like an error in the first concoction, spreads its ill influence through all our lives.

The soil is rich and would, if well cultivated, produce a noble harvest; if then the unskillful managers not only permit, but encourage noxious weeds, though we shall suffer by their neglect, yet they ought not in justice to blame any but themselves, if they reap the fruit of their own folly. Women are from their very infancy debarred those advantages, with the want of which they are afterwards reproached, and nursed up in those vices which will hereafter be upbraided to them. So partial are men as to expect brick where they afford no straw; and so abundantly civil as to take care we should make good that obliging epithet of *ignorant*, which out of an excess of good manners, they are pleased to bestow on us!

Having demonstrated the sorry state of women in her society, she proposes her remedy:

Now as to the Proposal, it is to erect a *monastery*, or if you will (to avoid giving offence to the scrupulous and injudicious, by names which though innocent in themselves, have been abused by superstitious practices) we will call it a *religious retirement*, and such as shall have a double aspect, being not only a retreat from the world for those who desire that advantage, but likewise, an institution and previous discipline to fit us to do the greatest good in it; such an institution as this (if I do not mightily deceive myself) would be the most probable method to amend the present, and improve the future age. For here, those who are convinced of the emptiness of earthly enjoyments, who are sick of the vanity of the world and its impertinencies, may find more substantial and satisfying entertainments and need not be confined to what they justly loathe. Those who are desirous to know and fortify their weak side, first do good to themselves that hereafter they may be capable of doing more good to others, or for their greater security are willing to avoid temptation, may get out of that danger which a continual stay in view of the enemy and the familiarity and unwearied application of the temptation may expose them to, and gain an opportunity to look into themselves, to be acquainted at home, and no longer the greatest strangers to their own hearts. Such as are willing in a more peculiar and undisturbed manner to attend the great business they came into the world about, the service of GOD and improvement of their own minds, may find a convenient and blissful recess from the noise and hurry of the world. A world so cumbersome, so infectious, that although through the grace of GOD, and their own strict watchfulness, they are kept from sinking down into its corruptions, 'twill however damp their flight to heaven, hinder them from attaining any eminent pitch of virtue.

You are therefore, Ladies, invited into a place, where you shall suffer no other confinement, but to be kept out of the road of sin: You shall not be deprived of your grandeur, but only exchange the vain pomps and pageantry of the world, empty titles and forms of state, for the true and solid greatness of being able to despise *them*. You will only quit the chat of insignificant people, for an ingenious conversation; the froth of flashy wit for real wisdom; idle tales for instructive discourses. The deceitful

flatteries of those who under pretence of loving and admiring
you, really served their *own* base ends, for the seasonable reproofs
and wholesome counsels of your hearty well-wishers and affectionate friends, which will procure you those perfections your
feigned lovers pretended you had and kept you from obtaining.
No uneasy task will be enjoined you, all your labour being only
to prepare for the highest degrees of that glory, the very lowest of
which is more than at present you are able to conceive, and the
prospect of it sufficient to outweigh all the pains of religion, were
there any in it, as really there is none. All that is required of you,
is only to be as happy as possibly you can and to make sure of a
felicity that will fill all the capacities of your souls! A happiness
which, when once you have tasted, you'll be fully convinced, you
could never do too much to obtain it; nor be too solicitous to
adorn your souls with such tempers and dispositions as will at
present make you in some measure such holy and heavenly creatures as you one day hope to be in a more perfect manner; without which qualifications you can neither reasonably *expect*, nor
are *capable* of enjoying the happiness of the life to come. Happy
Retreat! which will be the introducing you into such a *Paradise*
as your Mother *Eve* forfeited, where you shall feast on pleasures
that do not, like those of the world, disappoint your expectations,
pall your appetites, and by the disgust they give you, put you on
the fruitless search after new delights, which when obtained are
as empty as the former; but such as will make you truly happy
now, and prepare you to be *perfectly* so hereafter. . . . In fine, the
place to which you are invited will be a type and antipast of
Heaven, where your employment will be as there, to magnify GOD,
and to love one another, and to communicate that useful *knowledge*, which by the due improvement of your time in study and
contemplation you will obtain, and which, when obtained, will
afford you a much sweeter and durable delight than all those pitiful diversions, those revellings and amusements, which now
through your ignorance of better, appear the only grateful and
relishing entertainments.

But because we were not made for ourselves, nor can by any
means so effectually glorify GOD and do good to our own souls as
by doing offices of charity and beneficence to others, and to the

intent that every virtue, and the highest degrees of every virtue, may be exercised and promoted the most that may be, your retreat shall be so managed as not to exclude the good works of an *active*, from the pleasure and serenity of a *contemplative* life, but by a due mixture of both retain all the advantages and avoid the inconveniencies that attend either. It shall not so cut you off from the world as to hinder you from bettering and improving it, but rather qualify you to do it the greatest good, and be a seminary to stock the kingdom with pious and prudent ladies, whose good example, it is to be hoped, will so influence the rest of their sex that women may no longer pass for those little useless and impertinent animals which the ill conduct of too many has caused them to be mistaken for.

We have hitherto considered our retirement only in relation to religion, which is indeed its *main*, I may say its *only* design; nor can this be thought too contracting a word, since religion is the adequate business of our lives and, largely considered, takes in all we have to do, nothing being a fit employment for a rational creature which has not either a *direct* or *remote* tendency to this great and *only* end. But because, as we have all along observed, religion never appears in its true beauty but when it is accompanied with wisdom and discretion, and that without a good understanding, we can scarce be *truly*, but never *eminently* good, being liable to a thousand seductions and mistakes; for even the men themselves, if they have not a competent degree of knowledge, they are carried about with every wind of doctrine. Therefore, one great end of this institution shall be to expel that cloud of ignorance which custom has involved us in, to furnish our minds with a stock of solid and useful knowledge, that the souls of women may no longer be the only unadorned and neglected things. . . . Being the soul was created for the contemplation of truth, as well as for the fruition of good, is it not as cruel and unjust to preclude women from the knowledge of the one, as well as from the enjoyment of the other? Especially since the will is blind, and cannot choose but by the direction of the understanding; or to speak more properly, since the soul always *wills* according as she *understands*, so that if she *understands* amiss she *wills* amiss: And as exercise enlarges and exalts any faculty, so through want of using, it becomes cramped and lessened; if we make little or no use of our understandings we shall shortly have none to use, and the more contracted and unemployed the deliberating and directive power is, the more liable is the elective to unworthy and mischievous options. What is it but the want of an ingenious education that renders the generality of feminine conversations so insipid and foolish, and their solitude so *insupportable*? Learning is therefore necessary to render them more agreeable and useful in company and to furnish them with becoming entertainments when alone, that so they may not be driven to those miserable shifts which too many make use of to put off their time, that precious talent that never lies on the hands of a judicious person. And since our happiness in the next world depends so far on those dispositions which we carry along with us out of this that without a right habitude and temper of mind, we are not capable of felicity; and seeing our beatitude consists in the contemplation of the divine Truth and Beauty, as well as in the fruition of His Goodness, can ignorance be a fit preparative for Heaven? Is it likely that she whose understanding has been busied about nothing but froth and trifles should be capable of delighting herself in noble and sublime truths? Let such therefore as deny us the improvement of our intellectuals, either take up his paradox, who said, *That women have no souls,* which at this time a day, when they are allowed to brutes, would be as unphilosophical as it is unmannerly; or else let them permit us to cultivate and improve them. There is a sort of learning indeed which is worse than the greatest ignorance: A woman may study plays and romances all her days, and be a great deal more knowing, but never a jot the wiser. Such a knowledge as this serves only to instruct and put her forward in the practice of the greatest follies; yet how can they justly blame her, who forbid, or at least won't afford opportunity of better? A rational mind *will* be employed, it will never be satisfied in doing nothing; and if you neglect to furnish it with good materials, 'tis like to take up with such as come to hand.

We pretend not that women should teach in the church, or usurp authority where it is not allowed them; permit us only to understand our *own* duty, and not be forced to take it upon trust from others.   .   .   .

The ladies, I'm sure, have no reason to dislike this Proposal; but I know not how the men will resent it, to have their enclosure broke down, and women invited to taste of that Tree of Knowledge they have so long unjustly *monopolized*. But they must excuse me, if I be as partial to my own sex as they are to theirs, and think women as capable of learning as men are and that it becomes them as well. For I cannot imagine wherein the hurt lies if, instead of doing mischief to one another by an uncharitable and vain conversation, women be enabled to inform and instruct those of their own sex at least; the Holy Ghost having left it on record that Priscilla as well as her husband catechised the eloquent Apollos, and the great Apostle [Paul] found no fault with her.

> One of the most significant benefits of this institution will be providing women the opportunity to cultivate friendship, "a blessing, the purchase of which were richly worth all the world besides!":

That institution, therefore, must needs be highly beneficial, which both disposes us to be friends ourselves and helps to find them. But by friendship I do not mean anything like those intimacies that are about in the world, which are often combinations in evil, and at best but insignificant dearnesses, as little resembling true friendship as modern practice does primitive Christianity. But I intend by it the greatest usefulness, the most refined and disinterested benevolence, a love that thinks nothing within the bounds of power and duty too much to do or suffer for its beloved: And makes no distinction betwixt its friend and itself, except that in temporals it prefers her interest.   .   .   .

And if after so many spiritual advantages, it be convenient to mention temporals, here heiresses and persons of fortune may be kept secure from the rude attempts of designing men; and she who has more money than discretion need not curse her stars for being exposed a prey to bold, importunate and rapacious vultures. She will not here be inveigled and imposed on, will neither be bought nor sold, nor be forced to marry for her own quiet, when she has no inclination to it but what the being tired out with a restless importunity occasions. Or if she be disposed to marry, here she may remain in safety till a convenient match be offered by her friends, and be freed from the danger of a dishonourable one. Modesty requiring that a woman should not love before marriage, but only make choice of one whom she can love hereafter: She who has none but innocent affections being easily able to fix them where duty requires.

And though at first I proposed to myself to speak nothing in particular of the employment of the religious, yet to give a specimen how useful they will be to the world, I am now inclined to declare that it is designed a part of their business shall be to give the best education to the children of persons of quality, who shall be attended and instructed in lesser matters by meaner persons deputed to that office; but the forming of their minds shall be the particular care of those of their own rank, who cannot have a more pleasant and useful employment than to exercise and increase their own knowledge by instilling it into these young ones, who are most like to profit under such tutors. . . .

And when by the increase of their revenue, the religious are enabled to do such a work of charity, the education they design to bestow on the daughters of gentlemen who are fallen into decay will be no inconsiderable advantage to the nation. For hereby many souls will be preserved from great dishonours and put in a comfortable way of subsisting, being either received into the House, if they incline to it, or otherwise disposed of. It being supposed that prudent men will reckon the endowments they here acquire a sufficient dowry.

Finally, Astell answers possible objections to her Proposal:

If any object against a learned education that it will make women vain and assuming, and instead of correcting, increase their pride, I grant that a smattering in learning may; for it has this effect on the men: none so dogmatical and so forward to show their parts as your little *pretenders* to science. But I would not have the ladies content themselves with the *show*, my desire is that they should not rest till they obtain the *substance*. And then she who is most knowing will be forward to own with the wise Socrates, that she knows nothing: nothing that is matter of pride and ostentation, nothing but what is attended with so much ignorance and imperfection that it cannot reasonably elate and puff her up. The more she knows, she will be the less subject to talkativeness and its sister vices, because she discerns that the most difficult piece of learning is to know when to use and when to hold one's tongue and never to speak but to the purpose.

But the men, if they rightly understand their own interest, have no reason to oppose the ingenious education of the women, since 'twould go a great way towards reclaiming the men; great is the influence we have over them in their childhood, in which time, if a mother be discreet and knowing as well as devout, she has many opportunities of giving such a *form* and *season* to the tender mind of the child as will show its good effects through all the stages of his life. But though you should not allow her capable of doing *good*, 'tis certain she may do *hurt*: If she do not *make* the child, she has power to *mar* him, by suffering her fondness to get the better of discreet affection. But besides this, a good and prudent wife would wonderfully work on an ill man; he must be a brute indeed who could hold out against all those innocent arts, those gentle persuasives and obliging methods she would use to reclaim him. Piety is often offensive, when it is accompanied with indiscretion: but she who is as wise as good possesses such charms as can hardly fail of prevailing. Doubtless, her husband is a much happier man, and more likely to abandon all his ill courses, than he who has none to come home to but an ignorant, froward and fantastic creature. An ingenious conversation will make his life comfortable, and he who can be so well entertained at home needs not run into temptations in search of diversions abroad. The only danger is that the wife be more knowing than the husband; but if she be, 'tis his own fault, since he wants no opportunities of improvement; unless he be a natural *blockhead*, and then such an one will need a wise woman to govern him, whose prudence will conceal it from public observation and at once both cover and supply his defects. Give me leave therefore to hope that no gentleman who has honourable designs will henceforward decry knowledge and ingenuity in her he would pretend to honour: Or if he does, it may serve for a test to distinguish the feigned and unworthy from the real lover.

Part II of the *Proposal*, added in 1697, further develops and enforces the arguments of Part I:

As for those who think so contemptibly of such a considerable part of GOD's creation as to suppose that we were made for nothing else but to admire and do them service, and to make provision for the low concerns of an animal life, we pity their mistake, and can calmly bear their scoffs, for they do not express so much contempt of us as they do of our Maker; and therefore the reproach of such incompetent judges is not an injury but an honor to us.

The ladies I hope pass a truer estimate on themselves, and need not be told that they were made for nobler purposes. For though I would by no means encourage pride, yet I would not have them take a mean and groveling spirit for true humility. A being content with ignorance is really but a pretence, for the frame of our nature is such that it is impossible we should be so; even those very pretenders value themselves for some knowledge or other, though it be a trifling or mistaken one. She who makes the most grimace at a woman of sense, who employs all her little skill in endeavouring to render learning and ingenuity ridiculous, is yet very desirous to be thought knowing in a dress, in the management of an intrigue, in coquetry or good housewifery. If then either the nobleness or necessity of our nature unavoidably excites us to a desire of advancing, shall it be thought a fault to do it by pursuing the best things? and since we *will* value ourselves on somewhat or other, why should it not be on the most substantial ground? The humblest person that lives has some self-esteem, nor is it either fit or possible that any should be without it. Because we always neglect what we despise, we take no care of its preservation and improvement; and were we thoroughly possessed with a contempt of ourselves, we should abandon all care both of our temporal and eternal concerns, and burst with envy at our neighbours. The only difference therefore between the humble and the proud is this, that whereas the former does not prize herself on some imaginary excellency, or for anything that is not truly valuable; does not ascribe to herself what is her Maker's due, nor esteem herself on any other account but because she is GOD's workmanship, endowed by him with many excellent qualities and made capable of knowing and enjoying the sovereign and only Good; so that her self-esteem does not terminate in her *self* but in GOD, and she values herself only for GOD's sake. The proud on the contrary is mistaken both in her estimate of good, and in thinking it is her own; she values herself on things that have no real excellency, or which at least add none to her, and forgets from whose liberality she receives them: She does not employ them in the Donor's service, all her care is to raise herself, and she little considers that the most excellent things are distributed to others in an equal, perhaps in a greater measure than to herself, they have opportunities of advancing as well as she, and so long as she's puffed up by this tumor of mind, they do really excel her.

The men therefore may still enjoy their prerogatives for us, we mean not to entrench on any of their lawful privileges; our only contention shall be that they may not outdo us in promoting his glory who is Lord both of them and us; And by all that appears the generality will not oppose us in this matter, we shall not provoke them by striving to be better Christians. They may busy their heads with affairs of state, and spend their time and strength in recommending themselves to an uncertain master, or a more giddy multitude; our only endeavour shall be to be absolute monarchs in our own bosoms. They shall still if they please dispute about religion, let 'em only give us leave to understand and practise it. And whilst they have unrivaled the glory of speaking as *many* languages as Babel afforded, we only desire to express ourselves pertinently and judiciously in *one*. We will not vie with them in thumbing over authors, nor pretend to be walking libraries, provided they'll but allow us a competent knowl-

edge of the books of GOD, Nature I mean and the Holy Scriptures:
And whilst they accomplish themselves with the knowledge of the
world, and experiment all the pleasures and follies of it, we'll
aspire no further than to be intimately acquainted with our own
hearts. And sure the complaisant and good-natured sex will not
deny us this; nor can they who are so well assured of their own
merit entertain the least suspicion that we shall overtop them. It
is upon some other account therefore that they object against our
Proposal, but what that is I shall not pretend to guess, since they
do not think fit to speak out and declare it.

SOME REFLECTIONS UPON MARRIAGE, OCCASIONED
BY THE DUCHESS OF MAZARINE'S CASE

> Astell grimly describes the consequences of marrying
> unwisely, but finds that a wife has little likelihood of happi-
> ness even under the best conditions. A woman would do
> better to "set up for that peculiar [particular] coronet the
> ancient Fathers talked of"; that is, remain a virgin. The
> early Christians preferred virginity to marriage as a more vir-
> tuous and (erroneously, Astell would say) a more strenuous
> course of life.

And as men have little reason to expect happiness when they
marry only for the love of money, wit, or beauty, as has been
already shown, so much less can a woman expect a tolerable life
when she goes upon these considerations. Let the business be carried as prudently as it can be on the woman's side, a reasonable
man can't deny that she has by much the harder bargain, because
she puts herself entirely into her husband's power, and if the
matrimonial yoke be grievous, neither law nor custom afford her
that redress which a man obtains. He who has sovereign power
does not value the provocations of a rebellious subject; he knows
how to subdue him with ease, and will make himself obeyed: But
patience and submission are the only comforts that are left to a
poor people who groan under tyranny, unless they are strong
enough to break the yoke, to depose and abdicate, which, I

doubt, would not be allowed of here. For whatever may be said against passive obedience in another case, I suppose there's no man but likes it very well in this; how much soever arbitrary power may be disliked on a throne, not Milton, nor B. H[oadly], nor any of the advocates of resistance, would cry up liberty to poor *female slaves* or plead for the lawfulness of resisting a private tyranny.

If there be a disagreeableness of humours, this, in my mind, is harder to be borne than greater faults, as being a continual plague, and for the most part incurable. Other vices a man may grow weary of, or may be convinced of the evil of them, he may forsake them, or they him; but his humour and temper are seldom, if ever, put off. Ill-nature sticks to him from his youth to his grey hairs, and a boy that's humorous and proud makes a peevish, positive, and insolent old man. . . .

If therefore it be a woman's hard fate to meet with a disagreeable temper, and of all others the haughty, imperious, and self-conceited are the most so, she is as unhappy as anything in this world can make her. For when a wife's temper does not please, if she makes her husband uneasy, he can find entertainments abroad; he has a hundred ways of relieving himself; but neither prudence nor duty will allow a woman to fly out: her business and entertainment are at home; and though he makes it ever so uneasy to her, she must be content and make her best on't. She who elects a monarch for life, who gives him an authority she cannot recall, however he misapply it, who puts her fortune and person entirely in his power, nay, even the very desires of her heart, according to some learned casuists, so as that it is not lawful to will or desire anything but what he approves and allows, had need be very sure that she does not make a fool her head, nor a vicious man her guide and pattern; she had best stay till she can meet with one who has the government of his own passions and has duly regulated his own desires, since he is to have such an absolute power over hers. But he who dotes on a face, he who makes money his idol, he who is charmed with vain and empty wit, gives no such evidence, either of wisdom or goodness, that a woman of any tolerable sense should care to venture herself to his conduct.

Indeed, your fine gentleman's actions are nowadays such that, did not custom and the dignity of his sex give weight and authority to them, a woman that thinks twice might bless herself and say, Is this the Lord and Master to whom I am to promise love, honour and obedience? What can be the object of love but amiable qualities, the image of the Deity impressed upon a generous and godlike mind, a mind that is above this world, to be sure above all the vices, the tricks and baseness of it; a mind that is not full of itself, nor contracted to little private interests, but which, in imitation of that glorious pattern it endeavours to copy after, expands and diffuses itself to its utmost capacity in doing good. But this fine gentleman is quite of another strain, he is the reverse of this in every instance. He is, I confess, very fond of his own dear person, he sees very much in it to admire; his air and mien, his words and actions, every motion he makes, declare it; but they must have a judgment of his size, every whit as shallow, and a partiality as great as his own, who can be of his mind. How then can I love? And if not love, much less honour? Love may arise from pity, or a generous desire to make that lovely which as yet is not so, when we see any hopes of success in our endeavours of improving it; but honour supposes some excellent qualities already, something worth our esteem; but, alas! there is nothing more contemptible than this trifle of a man, this mere outside, whose mind is as base and mean as his external pomp is glittering. His office or title apart, to which some ceremonious observance must be paid for Order's sake, there's nothing in him that can command our respect. Strip him of equipage and fortune, and such things as only dazzle our eyes and imaginations but don't in any measure affect our reason or cause a reverence in our hearts, and the poor creature sinks beneath our notice, because not supported by real worth. And if a woman can neither love nor honour, she does ill in promising to obey, since she is like to have a crooked rule to regulate her actions.

A mere obedience, such as is paid only to authority, and not out of love and a sense of the justice and reasonableness of the command, will be of an uncertain tenure. As it can't but be uneasy to the person who pays it, so he who receives it will be sometimes disappointed when he expects to find it: For that woman must be endowed with a wisdom and goodness much above what we suppose the sex capable of, I fear much greater than any man can pretend to, who can so constantly conquer her passions and divest herself even of innocent self-love, as to give up the cause when she is in the right, and to submit her enlightened reason to the imperious dictates of a blind will and wild imagination, even when she clearly perceives the ill consequences of it, the imprudence, nay, folly and madness of such a conduct.

And if a woman runs such a risk when she marries prudently, according to the opinion of the world, that is, when she permits herself to be disposed of to a man equal to her in birth, education and fortune and as good as the most of his neighbours (for if none were to marry but men of strict virtue and honour, I doubt the world would be but thinly peopled), if at the very best her lot is hard, what can she expect who is sold or any otherwise betrayed into mercenary hands, to one who is in all, or most respects, unequal to her? A lover who comes upon what is called equal terms makes no very advantageous proposal to the lady he courts, and to whom he seems to be an humble servant. For under many sounding compliments, words that have nothing in them, this is his true meaning: He wants one to manage his family, an housekeeper, one whose interest it will be not to wrong him, and in whom therefore he can put greater confidence than in any he can hire for money. One who may breed his children, taking all the care and trouble of their education, to preserve his name and family. One whose beauty, wit, or good humour and agreeable conversation will entertain him at home when he has been contradicted and disappointed abroad, who will do him that justice the ill-natured world denies him; that is, in anyone's language but his own, soothe his pride and flatter his vanity, by having always so much good sense as to be on his side, to conclude him in the right, when others are so ignorant or so rude as to deny it. Who will not be blind to his merit nor contradict his will and pleasure, but make it her business, her very ambition to content him, whose softness and gentle compliance will calm his passions, to whom he may safely disclose his troublesome thoughts, and in her breast discharge his cares, whose duty, submission and observance will heal those wounds other people's opposition or neglect have given him. In a word, one whom he can entirely govern, and consequently may form her to his will and liking, who must be his for life, and therefore cannot quit his service, let him treat her how he will. . . .

But how can a woman scruple entire subjection, how can she forbear to admire the worth and excellency of the superior sex, if she at all considers it! Have not all the great actions that have been performed in the world been done by men? Have not they founded empires and overturned them? Do not they make laws and continually repeal and amend them? Their vast minds lay kingdoms waste, no bounds or measures can be prescribed to their desires. War and peace depend on them; they form cabals and have the wisdom and courage to get over all the rubs, the petty restraints which honour and conscience may lay in the way of their desired grandeur. What is it they cannot do? They make worlds and ruin them, form systems of universal nature and dispute eternally about them; their pen gives worth to the most trifling controversy; nor can a fray be inconsiderable if they have drawn their swords in't. All that the wise man pronounces is an oracle, and every word the witty speaks, a jest. It is a woman's happiness to hear, admire and praise them, especially if a little ill-nature keeps them at any time from bestowing due applauses on each other! And if she aspires no further, she is thought to be in her proper sphere of action; she is as wise and as good as can be expected from her!

She then who marries ought to lay it down for an indisputable maxim, that her husband must govern absolutely and entirely, and that she has nothing else to do but to please and obey. She must not attempt to divide his authority, or so much as dispute it; to struggle with her yoke will only make it gall the more, but must believe him wise and good, and in all respects the best; at least he must be so to her. She who can't do this is no way fit to be a wife; she may set up for that peculiar coronet the ancient Fathers talked of, but is not qualified to receive that great reward which attends the eminent exercise of humility and self-denial, patience and resignation, the duties that a wife is called to.

But some refractory woman perhaps will say, how can this be? Is it possible for her to believe him wise and good who by a thousand demonstrations convinces her, and all the world, of the contrary? Did the bare name of husband confer sense on a man, and the mere being in authority infallibly qualify him for government, much might be done. But since a wise man and a husband are not terms convertible, and how loath soever one is to own it, matter of fact won't allow us to deny that the head many times stands in need of the inferior's brains to manage it, she must beg leave to be excused from such high thoughts of her sovereign, and if she submits to his power, it is not so much reason as necessity that compels her.

Now of how little force soever this objection may be in other respects, methinks it is strong enough to prove the necessity of a good education, and that men never mistake their true interest more than when they endeavour to keep women in ignorance. Could they indeed deprive them of their natural good sense at the same time they deny them the true improvement of it, they might compass their end; otherwise natural sense unassisted may run into a false track and serve only to punish him justly, who would not allow it to be useful to himself or others. If man's authority be justly established, the more sense a woman has, the more reason she will find to submit to it; if according to the tradition of our fathers (who having had *possession* of the pen, thought they had also the best *right* to it) women's understanding is but small, and man's partiality adds no weight to the observation, ought not the more care to be taken to improve them? How it agrees with the justice of men we inquire not, but certainly Heaven is abundantly more equitable than to enjoin women the hardest task, and give them the least strength to perform it. And if men, learned, wise, and discreet as they are, who have, as is said, all the advantages of nature, and without controversy have, or may have, all the assistance of art, are so far from acquitting themselves as they ought, from living according to that reason and excellent understanding they so much boast of, can it be expected that a woman, who is reckoned silly enough in herself, at least comparatively, and whom men take care to make yet more so, can it be expected that she should constantly perform so difficult a duty as entire subjection, to which corrupt Nature is so averse?

If the great and wise Cato, a *man*, a man of no ordinary firmness and strength of mind, a man who was esteemed as an oracle, and by the philosophers and great men of his nation equaled even to the gods themselves, if he, with all his Stoical principles, was not able to bear the sight of a triumphant conqueror (who perhaps would have insulted, and perhaps would not), but out of a cowardly fear of an insult, ran to death to secure him from it; can it be thought that an ignorant weak woman should have patience to bear a continual outrage and insolence all the days of her life? Unless you will suppose her a *very ass*, but then remember what the Italians say, to quote them once more, since being *very* husbands they may be presumed to have some authority in this case, *An ass, though slow, if provoked, will kick.*

We never observe, or perhaps make sport with, the ill effects of a bad education, till it comes to touch us home in the ill conduct of a sister, a daughter, or wife. Then the women must be blamed, their folly is exclaimed against, when all this while it was the wise man's fault, who did not set a better guard on those who, according to him, stand in so much need of one. A young gentleman, as a celebrated author tells us, ought above all things to be acquainted with the state of the world, the ways and humours, the follies, the cheats, the faults of the age he is fallen into; he should by degrees be informed of the vice in fashion and warned of the application and design of those who will make it their business to corrupt him, should be told the arts they use and the trains they lay, be prepared to be shocked by some and caressed by others; warned who are like to oppose, who to mislead, who to undermine, and who to serve him. He should be instructed how to know and distinguish them, where he should let them see, and when dissemble the knowledge of them and their aims and workings. Our author is much in the right, and not to disparage any other accomplishments which are useful in their kind, this will turn to more account than any language or philosophy, art or science, or any other piece of good-breeding

and fine education that can be taught him, which are no otherwise excellent than as they contribute to this, as this does above
all things to the making him a wise, a virtuous and useful man.

And it is not less necessary that a young lady should receive
the like instructions; whether or no her temptations be fewer, her
reputation and honour however are to be more nicely preserved;
they may be ruined by a little ignorance or indiscretion, and then
though she has kept her innocence, and so is secured as to the
next world, yet she is in a great measure lost to this. A woman
cannot be too watchful, too apprehensive of her danger, nor keep
at too great a distance from it, since man, whose wisdom and
ingenuity is so much superior to hers! condescends for his interest
sometimes, and sometimes by way of diversion, to lay snares for
her. For though all men are *virtuosi*, philosophers and politicians, in comparison of the ignorant and illiterate women, yet
they don't all pretend to be saints, and 'tis no great matter to
them if women, who were born to be their slaves, be now and
then ruined for their entertainment.

But according to the rate that young women are educated,
according to the way their time is spent, they are destined to folly
and impertinence, to say no worse, and, which is yet more inhuman, they are blamed for that ill conduct they are not suffered to
avoid and reproached for those faults they are in a manner forced
into; so that if Heaven has bestowed any sense on them, no other
use is made of it than to leave them without excuse. So much,
and no more, of the world is shown them than serves to weaken
and corrupt their minds, to give them wrong notions, and busy
them in mean pursuits; to disturb, not to regulate their passions;
to make them timorous and dependent, and, in a word, fit for
nothing else but to act a farce for the diversion of their gover-
nors.

Even men themselves improve no otherwise than according
to the aim they take and the end they propose, and he whose
designs are but little and mean, will be the same himself. Though
ambition, as 'tis usually understood, is a foolish, not to say a base
and pitiful vice, yet the aspirings of the soul after true glory are
so much its nature that it seems to have forgot itself, and to

degenerate, if it can forbear; and perhaps the great secret of education lies in affecting the soul with a lively sense of what is truly its perfection and exciting the most ardent desires after it.

But, alas! what poor woman is ever taught that she should have a higher design than to get her a husband? Heaven will fall in of course, and if she makes but an obedient and dutiful wife, she cannot miss of it. A husband indeed is thought by both sexes so very valuable that scarce a man who can keep himself clean and make a bow, but thinks he is good enough to pretend to any woman; no matter for the difference of birth or fortune, a husband is such a wonder-working name as to make an equality, or something more, whenever it is obtained.

Unfortunately, Astell concludes, this social conditioning has prevented most women from recognizing their degrading subjection.

Women . . . are for the most part wise enough to love their chains, and to discern how very becomingly they fit. They think as humbly of themselves as their masters can wish, with respect to the other sex; but in regard to their own, they have a spice of masculine ambition; every one would lead, and none would follow. Both sexes being too apt to envy and too backward in emulating, and take more delight in detracting from their neighbour's virtue than in improving their own. And therefore, as to those women who find themselves born for slavery, and are so sensible of their own meanness as to conclude it impossible to attain to anything excellent, since they are, or ought to be best acquainted with their own strength and genius, she's a fool who would attempt their deliverance or improvement. No, let them enjoy the great honour and felicity of their tame, submissive and depending temper! Let the men applaud, and let them glory in this wonderful humility! Let them receive the flatteries and grimaces of the other sex, live unenvied by their own, and be as much beloved as one such woman can afford to love another! Let them enjoy the glory of treading in the footsteps of their predecessors, and of having the prudence to avoid that audacious attempt of soaring beyond their sphere! Let them huswife or play, dress, and be pretty entertaining company! Or, which is better, relieve the poor to ease their own compassions, read pious books, say their prayers, and go to church, because they have been taught and used to do so, without being able to give a better reason for their faith and practice! Let them not by any means aspire at being women of understanding, because no man can endure a woman of superior sense, or would treat a reasonable woman civilly but that he thinks he stands on higher ground and that she is so wise as to make exceptions in his favour and to take her measures by his directions; they may pretend to sense, indeed, since mere pretences only render one the more ridiculous! Let them, in short, be what is called *very* women, for this is most acceptable to all sorts of men; or let them aim at the title of *good devout* women, since some men can bear with this; but let them not judge of the sex by their own scantling: For the great Author of Nature and Fountain of all Perfection never designed that the mean and imperfect, but that the most complete and excellent of His creatures in every kind, should be the standard to the rest.

Bibliographical Note

Mary Astell published *Letters Concerning the Love of God* (1695), *A Serious Proposal to the Ladies for the Advancement of Their True and Greatest Interest* (1694), *A Serious Proposal to the Ladies: Part II* (1697), *Some Reflections Upon Marriage, Occasioned by the Duke and Duchess of Mazarine's Case* (1700), *Moderation Truly Stated* (1704), *A Fair Way with the Dissenters and Their Patrons* (1704), *An Impartial Enquiry Into the Causes of Rebellion and Civil War in This Kingdom* (1704), *The Christian Religion as Professed by a Daughter of the Church of England* (1705), and *Bart'lemy Fair or an Enquiry After Wit* (1709).

The only book about her is Florence M. Smith, *Mary Astell* (New York: Columbia University Press, 1916).

LADY MARY
WORTLEY MONTAGU

Lady Mary Pierrepoint (1689–1762) was early introduced to the most brilliant circles of London society. Before she was eight years old, her father displayed her wit and beauty to his friends, who included Joseph Addison, Richard Steele, and William Congreve. But she was left to educate herself, reading voluminously in her father's library and even teaching herself Latin. After a clandestine and troubled courtship, she eloped with Edward Wortley Montagu, a rising politician, in 1712. She had two children, a son who turned out badly and a daughter who married John Stuart, Earl of Bute, who was to become Prime Minister under George III.

While Wortley pursued his career at the court of George I, Lady Mary cultivated literature and literary society. She wrote and circulated essays and poems, such as five clever "town eclogues" satirizing the fashionable world, but would never have thought of herself as a professional writer. Her warmest friendship was with Alexander Pope, but after some years they quarreled bitterly, and his later poems are peppered with savage references to her under the name of Sappho.

When her husband was named ambassador to Turkey in 1716, Lady Mary accompanied him, sending home a series of fascinating letters (which, like Winchilsea, she left to be published after her death). Mary Astell wrote a Preface for the collection in 1724, pointing out their superior originality to travel accounts written by men and urging women to lay aside envy and "be pleased that a *woman* triumphs." Montagu also learned the Turkish method of inoculation for smallpox (the disease had left her badly scarred), which she applied to her own son and publicized on her return to England, despite the opposition of the medical establishment. In 1737–38 she conducted a periodical in support of Sir Robert Walpole's ministry called *The Nonsense of Common-Sense*; the sixth of its nine numbers is a feminist essay suggesting the influence of Astell.

At this time she fell deeply in love with a handsome bisexual Italian, Count Francesco Algarotti; this passion may have prompted her to terminate her marriage, which had long been obviously incompatible. She and Wortley separated by mutual consent, apparently on condition that she stay out of England. She settled in Italy, far away from her beloved daughter, and never saw her grandchildren until her husband's death in 1761. Her most touching and interesting letters are the ones in which she tried to keep up her relationship with her daughter's family.

The first letter given here is to her girlhood friend Philippa Mundy; the next three describe life in Turkey; the fourth relates London gossip to amuse her sister, Lady Mar, who was sinking into depression; and in the last three she advises her daughter about educating an intellectual granddaughter and comments on contemporary literature. The three "Turkish Letters" have been revised by Montagu with an eye to eventual publication.

TO PHILIPPA MUNDY (10 January 1713)

You will be convinced, my dear Phil, that absence and distance can make no alteration in my heart, or diminution of your power there, by my sudden answer to your obliging letter, notwithstanding the impediments to writing, arising from company, or my own indisposition, which renders it almost always uneasy to me.

You ask my advice in a matter too difficult, but since you ask it, my friendship obliges me to give it to the best of my understanding. You have not made your case very clear, but I think you ask whether it would conduce most to your happiness to comply with your relations, in taking a man whose person you dislike, or to dispose of yourself according to your inclination. By that expression of a thorough contempt of the pomps and vanities of this wicked world, I suppose your inclination is in favor of one unequal in point of fortune to him proposed by your father. I know there is nothing more natural than for a heart in love to imagine nothing more easy than to reduce all expenses to a very narrow compass. If you like a man of a £500 per annum, I am sure you imagine you can live without one thought of equipage, or that proportion of attendance, new clothes, etc., that you have been used to. But, my dear, can you be very sure of this? The cares, the self denial, and the novelty that you will find in that manner of living, will it never be uneasy to you? Accidental losses, thousands of unforeseen chances, may make you repent a hasty action, never to be undone. When time and cares have changed you to a downright housekeeper, will you not try,

> Though then, alas, that trial be too late,
> To find your father's hospitable gate,
> And seats where ease and plenty brooding sate,
> Those seats which long excluded you may mourn,
> That gate for ever barred to your return?

My dear Phil, my kindness for you makes me carry it very far, and beg you to look a little on the other side. If the gentleman

proposed to you has really no other fault but a disagreeable
person, if his conversation is to be liked, his principles to be
esteemed, and there is nothing loathsome in his form, nor no dis-
proportion in your ages, if all your dislike is founded on a dis-
pleasing mixture of features, it cannot last long. There is no
figure that after the eyes have been accustomed to, does not
become pleasing, or at least not otherwise. I fancy it is him that I
danced with at N.; if so, I cannot commend his person; but if his
understanding is to be valued, the progress from esteem to love is
shorter and easier than it is generally imagined.

However, after all I have said, if the difference between your
choice and your father's is only between a great estate and a com-
petency, 'tis better to be privately happy than splendidly miserable. The reputation of having acted prudently will be no comfort. Follow your inclination, but in the first place remember,
though 'tis easy to be without superfluities, 'tis impossible to be
without necessaries, and as the world is made (and I see no prospect of its being reformed) there are some superfluities become
necessaries. You can be without six horses, you can't be without a
coach; you can be without laced liveries, you can't be without
footmen. Consider over these things calmly, but if you have a
beloved lover with an easy fortune, consider also 'tis possible to
be very happy without the rank and show of Mr. Ch[ester]'s
wife, and (as an experienced person) I advise you to consult
chiefly and firstly if you can be pleased and secondly the world.
But if both is impossible, please yourself, and believe from my
experience there is no state so happy as with a man you like.— I
should not be so free in giving my opinion, dear Phil, but
through an entire zeal for your happiness, which I heartily wish
for, and conclude my letter with a seasonable remembrance,

> Now is your hour, or to comply or shun,
> Better not do the deed, than weep it done.

If you would avoid Mr. C. only because he is not well made,
don't avoid him; if you would marry another only because you
like him, don't marry him.

One word of your little friend, and I have done. If you was to meet, she would be as fond as ever. There are some people no more made for friends than politicians.

TO LADY _____ (1 April 1717)

I am now got into a new world where every thing I see appears to me a change of scene, and I write to your Ladyship with some content of mind, hoping at least that you will find the charm of novelty in my letters and no longer reproach me that I tell you nothing extraordinary. I won't trouble you with a relation of our tedious journey, but I must not omit what I saw remarkable at Sophia, one of the most beautiful towns in the Turkish Empire and famous for its hot baths that are resorted to both for diversion and health. I stopped here one day on purpose to see them. Designing to go incognito, I hired a Turkish coach. These voitures are not at all like ours, but much more convenient for the country, the heat being so great that glasses would be very troublesome. They are made a good deal in the manner of the Dutch coaches, having wooden lattices painted and gilded, the inside being painted with baskets and nosegays of flowers, inter-mixed commonly with little poetical mottos. They are covered all over with scarlet cloth, lined with silk and very often richly embroidered and fringed. This covering entirely hides the per-sons in them, but may be thrown back at pleasure and the ladies peep through the lattices. They hold four people very conven-iently, seated on cushions, but not raised.

In one of these covered wagons I went to the bagnio about ten o'clock. It was already full of women. It is built of stone in the shape of a dome with no windows but in the roof, which gives light enough. There were five of these domes joined together, the outmost being less than the rest and serving only as a hall where the portress stood at the door. Ladies of quality gen-erally give this woman the value of a crown or ten shillings, and I did not forget that ceremony. The next room is a very large one, paved with marble, and all round it raised two sofas of marble, one above another. There were four fountains of cold water in this room, falling first into marble basins and then running on the floor in little channels made for that purpose, which carried the streams into the next room, something less than this, with the same sort of marble sofas, but so hot with steams of sulphur proceeding from the baths joining to it, 'twas impossible to stay there with one's clothes on. The two other domes were the hot baths, one of which had cocks of cold water turning into it to temper it to what degree of warmth the bathers have a mind to.

I was in my travelling habit, which is a riding dress, and certainly appeared very extraordinary to them, yet there was not one of 'em that showed the least surprise or impertinent curiosity, but received me with all the obliging civility possible. I know no European court where the ladies would have behaved themselves in so polite a manner to a stranger.

I believe in the whole there were two hundred women and yet none of those disdainful smiles or satiric whispers that never fail in our assemblies when anybody appears that is not dressed exactly in fashion. They repeated over and over to me, "Uzelle, pek uzelle," which is nothing but, "Charming, very charming." The first sofas were covered with cushions and rich carpets, on which sat the ladies, and on the second their slaves behind 'em, but without any distinction of rank by their dress, all being in the state of nature, that is, in plain English, stark naked, without any beauty or defect concealed, yet there was not the least wanton smile or immodest gesture amongst 'em. They walked and moved with the same majestic grace which Milton describes of our general mother. There were many amongst them as exactly proportioned as ever any goddess was drawn by the pencil of Guido or Titian, and most of their skins shiningly white, only adorned by their beautiful hair divided into many tresses hanging on their shoulders, braided either with pearl or riband, perfectly representing the figures of the Graces. I was here convinced of the truth of a reflection that I had often made, that if 'twas the fashion to go naked, the face would be hardly observed. I perceived that the ladies with the finest skins and most delicate shapes had the greatest share of my admiration, though their faces were sometimes less beautiful than those of their companions. To tell you the truth, I had wickedness enough to wish secretly that Mr. Jervas could have been there invisible. I fancy it would have very much improved his art to see so many fine women naked in different postures, some in conversation, some working, others drinking coffee or sherbet, and many negligently lying on their cushions while their slaves (generally pretty girls of seventeen or eighteen) were employed in braiding their hair in several pretty manners. In short, 'tis the women's coffee house, where all the news of the town is told, scandal invented, etc. They generally take this diversion once a week, and stay there at least four or five hours without getting cold by immediate coming out of the hot bath into the cool room, which was very surprising to me. The lady that seemed the most considerable amongst them entreated me to sit by her and would fain have undressed me for the bath. I excused myself with some difficulty, they being all so earnest in persuading me. I was at last forced to open my skirt and show them my stays, which satisfied 'em very well, for I saw they believed I was so locked up in that machine that it was not in my own power to open it, which contrivance they attributed to my husband. I was charmed with their civility and beauty and should have been very glad to pass more time with them, but Mr. W[ortley] resolving to pursue his journey the next morning early, I was in haste to see the ruins of Justinian's church, which did not afford me so agreeable a prospect as I had left, being little more than a heap of stones.

Adieu, Madam. I am sure I have now entertained you with an account of such a sight as you never saw in your life and what no book of travels could inform you of. 'Tis no less than death for a man to be found in one of these places.

TO SARAH CHISWELL (1 April 1717)

In my opinion, dear S[arah], I ought rather to quarrel with you for not answering my Nijmegan letter of August till December, than to excuse my not writing again till now. I am sure there is on my side a very good excuse for silence, having gone such tiresome land journeys, though I don't find the conclusion of 'em so bad as you seem to imagine. I am very easy here and not in the

solitude you fancy me; the great quantity of Greek, French, Eng-
ish and Italians that are under our protection make their court
to me from morning till night, and I'll assure you are many of
'em very fine ladies, for there is no possibility for a Christian to
live easily under this government but by the protection of an
ambassador, and the richer they are the greater their danger.

Those dreadful stories you have heard of the plague have
very little foundation in truth. I own I have much ado to recon-
cile myself to the sound of a word which has always given me
such terrible ideas, though I am convinced there is little more in
it than a fever, as a proof of which we passed through two or
three towns most violently infected. In the very next house where
we lay, in one of 'em, two persons died of it. Luckily for me I was
so well deceived that I knew nothing of the matter, and I was
made believe that our second cook who fell ill there had only a
great cold. However, we left our doctor to take care of him, and
yesterday they both arrived here in good health and I am now let
into the secret that he has had the plague. There are many that
'scape of it, neither is the air ever infected. I am persuaded it
would be as easy to root it out here as out of Italy and France,
but it does so little mischief, they are not very solicitous about it
and are content to suffer this distemper instead of our variety,
which they are utterly unacquainted with.

A propos of distempers, I am going to tell you a thing that I
am sure will make you wish yourself here. The smallpox, so fatal
and so general amongst us, is here entirely harmless by the invention of engrafting (which is the term they give it). There is a set
of old women who make it their business to perform the operation. Every autumn in the month of September, when the great
heat is abated, people send to one another to know if any of their
family has a mind to have the smallpox. They make parties for
this purpose, and when they are met (commonly fifteen or six-
teen together) the old woman comes with a nutshell full of the
matter of the best sort of smallpox and asks what veins you please
to have opened. She immediately rips open that you offer to her
with a large needle (which gives you no more pain than a
common scratch) and puts into the vein as much venom as can
lie upon the head of her needle, and after binds up the little

wound with a hollow bit of shell, and in this manner opens four or five veins. The Grecians have commonly the superstition of opening one in the middle of the forehead, in each arm and on the breast to mark the sign of the cross, but this has a very ill effect, all these wounds leaving little scars, and is not done by those that are not superstitious, who choose to have them in the legs or that part of the arm that is concealed. The children or young patients play together all the rest of the day and are in perfect health till the eighth. Then the fever begins to seize 'em and they keep their beds two days, very seldom three. They have very rarely above twenty or thirty in their faces, which never mark, and in eight days time they are as well as before their illness. Where they are wounded there remain running sores during the distemper, which I don't doubt is a great relief to it. Every year thousands undergo this operation, and the French Ambassador says pleasantly that they take the smallpox here by way of diversion as they take the waters in other countries. There is no example of anyone that has died in it, and you may believe I am very well satisfied of the safety of the experiment since I intend to try it on my dear little son. I am patriot enough to take pains to bring this useful invention into fashion in England, and I should not fail to write to some of our doctors very particularly about it if I knew any one of 'em that I thought had virtue enough to destroy such a considerable branch of their revenue for the good of mankind, but that distemper is too beneficial to them not to expose to all their resentment the hardy wight that should undertake to put an end to it. Perhaps if I live to return I may, however, have courage to war with 'em. Upon this occasion, admire the heroism in the heart of your friend.

TO THE COUNTESS OF _____ (May 1718)

Your Ladyship may be assured I received yours with very great pleasure. I am very glad to hear that our friends are in good health, particularly Mr. Congreve, who I hear was ill of the gout. I am now preparing to leave Constantinople, and perhaps you will accuse me of hypocrisy when I tell you 'tis with regret, but I am used to the air and have learnt the language. I am easy here, and as much as I love travelling, I tremble at the inconveniences attending so great a journey with a numerous family and a little infant hanging at the breast. However, I endeavour upon this occasion to do as I have hitherto done in all the odd turns of my life, turn 'em, if I can, to my diversion. In order to this, I ramble every day, wrapped up in my *ferigé* and *asmak*, about Constantinople and amuse myself with seeing all that is curious in it. I know you'll expect this declaration should be followed with some account of what I have seen, but I am in no humour to copy what has been writ so often over. To what purpose should I tell you that Constantinople was the ancient Byzantium; that 'tis at present the conquest of a race of people supposed Scythians; that there are five or six thousand mosques in it; that Santa Sophia was founded by Justinian, etc? I'll assure you 'tis not want of learning that I forbear writing all these bright things. I could also, with little trouble, turn over Knolles and Sir Paul Rycaut to give you a list of Turkish emperors, but I will not tell you what you may find in every author that has writ of this country.

I am more inclined, out of a true female spirit of contradiction, to tell you the falsehood of a great part of what you find in authors; as, for example, the admirable Mr. Hill, who so gravely asserts that he saw in Santa Sophia a sweating pillar very balsamic for disordered heads. There is not the least tradition of any such matter, and I suppose it was revealed to him in vision during his wonderful stay in the Egyptian catacombs, for I am sure he never heard of any such miracle here. 'Tis also very pleasant to observe how tenderly he and all his brethren voyage-writers lament the miserable confinement of the Turkish ladies, who are (perhaps) freer than any ladies in the universe, and are the only women in the world that lead a life of uninterrupted pleasure, exempt from cares, their whole time being spent in visiting, bathing, or the agreeable amusement of spending money and inventing new fashions. A husband would be thought mad that exacted any degree of economy from his wife, whose expenses are no way limited but by her own fancy. 'Tis his business to get money and hers to spend it, and this noble prerogative extends itself to the very meanest of the sex. Here is a fellow that carries

embroidered handkerchiefs upon his back to sell, as miserable a
figure as you may suppose such a mean dealer, yet I'll assure you
his wife scorns to wear anything less than cloth of gold, has her
ermine furs, and a very handsome set of jewels for her head.
They go abroad when and where they please. 'Tis true they have
no public places but the bagnios, and there can only be seen by
their own sex; however, that is a diversion they take great pleasure in.

I was three days ago at one of the finest in the town and had
the opportunity of seeing a Turkish bride received there and all
the ceremonies used on that occasion, which made me recollect
the epithalamium of Helen by Theocritus, and it seems to me
that the same customs have continued ever since. All the she-
friends, relations and acquaintance of the two families newly
allied meet at the bagnio. Several others go out of curiosity, and I
believe there were that day at least two hundred women. Those
that were or had been married, placed themselves round the
room on the marble sofas, but the virgins very hastily threw off
their clothes and appeared without other ornament or covering
than their own long hair braided with pearl or riband. Two of
them met the bride at the door, conducted by her mother and
another grave relation. She was a beautiful maid of about seventeen, very richly dressed and shining with jewels, but was presently reduced by them to the state of nature. Two others filled
silver gilt pots with perfume and begun the procession, the rest
following in pairs to the number of thirty. The leaders sung an
epithalamium answered by the others in chorus, and the two last
led the fair bride, her eyes fixed on the ground with a charming
affectation of modesty. In this order they marched round the
three large rooms of the bagnio. 'Tis not easy to represent to you
the beauty of this sight, most of them being well proportioned
and white skinned, all of them perfectly smooth and polished by
the frequent use of bathing. After having made their tour, the
bride was again led to every matron round the rooms, who
saluted her with a compliment and a present, some of jewels,
others pieces of stuff, handkerchiefs, or little gallantries of that
nature, which she thanked them for by kissing their hands.

I was very well pleased with having seen this ceremony, and

you may believe me that the Turkish ladies have at least as much
wit and civility, nay, liberty, as ladies amongst us. 'Tis true the
same customs that give them so many opportunities of gratifying
their evil inclinations (if they have any) also put it very fully in
the power of their husbands to revenge them if they are discovered, and I don't doubt but they suffer sometimes for their indis-
cretions in a very severe manner. About two months ago there
was found at daybreak not very far from my house the bleeding
body of a young woman, naked, only wrapped in a coarse sheet,
with two wounds with a knife, one in her side and another in her
breast. She was not yet quite cold, and so surprisingly beautiful
that there were few men in Pera that did not go to look upon
her, but it was not possible for anybody to know her, no woman's
face being known. She was supposed to be brought in dead of
night from the Constantinople side and laid there. Very little
enquiry was made about the murderer, and the corpse privately
buried without noise. Murder is never pursued by the King's
officers as with us. 'Tis the business of the next relations to
revenge the dead person; and if they like better to compound the
matter for money (as they generally do) there is no more said of
it. One would imagine this defect in their government should
make such tragedies very frequent, yet they are extremely rare,
which is enough to prove the people not naturally cruel, neither
do I think in many other particulars they deserve the barbarous
character we give them.

I am well acquainted with a Christian woman of quality who
made it her choice to live with a Turkish husband, and is a very
agreeable sensible lady. Her story is so extraordinary I cannot forbear relating it, but I promise you it shall be in as few words as I
can possibly express it. She is a Spaniard, and was at Naples with
her family when that kingdom was part of the Spanish dominion.
Coming from thence in a felucca, accompanied by her brother,
they were attacked by the Turkish Admiral, boarded and taken;
and now, how shall I modestly tell you the rest of her adventure?
The same accident happened to her that happened to the fair
Lucretia so many years before her, but she was too good a Christian to kill herself as that heathenish Roman did. The Admiral
was so much charmed with the beauty and long-suffering of the

fair captive that as his first compliment he gave immediate liberty to her brother and attendants, who made haste to Spain and in a few months sent the sum of £4,000 sterling as a ransom for his sister. The Turk took the money, which he presented to her, and told her she was at liberty, but the lady very discreetly weighed the different treatment she was likely to find in her native country. Her Catholic relations, as the kindest thing they could do for her in her present circumstances, would certainly confine her to a nunnery for the rest of her days. Her infidel lover was very handsome, very tender, fond of her, and lavished at her feet all the Turkish magnificence. She answered him very resolutely that her liberty was not so precious to her as her honour, that he could no way restore that but by marrying her. She desired him to accept the ransom as her portion and give her the satisfaction of knowing no man could boast of her favours without being her husband. The Admiral was transported at this kind offer and sent back the money to her relations, saying he was too happy in her possession. He married her and never took any other wife, and (as she says herself) she never had any reason to repent the choice she made. He left her some years after one of the richest widows in Constantinople, but there is no remaining honourably a single woman, and that consideration has obliged her to marry the present Capitan Bassa (i.e. Admiral), his successor. I am afraid you'll think that my friend fell in love with her ravisher, but I am willing to take her word for it that she acted wholly on principles of honour, though I think she might be reasonably touched at his generosity, which is very often found amongst the Turks of rank.

'Tis a degree of generosity to tell the truth, and 'tis very rare that any Turk will assert a solemn falsehood. I don't speak of the lowest sort, for as there is a great deal of ignorance, there is very little virtue amongst them; and false witnesses are much cheaper than in Christendom, those wretches not being punished (even when they are publicly detected) with the rigour they ought to be. Now I am speaking of their law, I don't know whether I have ever mentioned to you one custom peculiar to this country. I mean adoption, very common amongst the Turks and yet more amongst the Greeks and Armenians. Not having it in their power

to give their estates to a friend or distant relation to avoid its falling into the Grand Signor's treasury, when they are not likely to
have children of their own they choose some pretty child of either
sex amongst the meanest people, and carry the child and its parents before the cadi, and there declare they receive it for their
heir. The parents at the same time renounce all future claim to
it, a writing is drawn and witnessed, and a child thus adopted
cannot be disinherited. Yet I have seen some common beggars
that have refused to part with their children in this manner to
some of the richest amongst the Greeks; so powerful is the
instinctive fondness natural to parents! though the adopting
fathers are generally very tender to these children of their souls,
as they call them. I own this custom pleases me much better than
our absurd following our name. Methinks 'tis much more reasonable to make happy and rich an infant whom I educate after my
own manner, brought up (in the Turkish phrase) upon my
knees, and who has learnt to look upon me with a filial respect,
than to give an estate to a creature without other merit or relation to me than by a few letters. Yet this is an absurdity we see
frequently practised. . . .

TO LADY MAR (23 June 1727)

I am always pleased to hear from you (dear Sister), particularly when you tell me you are well. I believe you'll find upon the
whole my sense is right, that air, exercise and company are the
best medicines, and physic and retirement good for nothing but
to break hearts and spoil constitutions.

I was glad to hear Mr. Rémond's history from you, though
the newspaper had given it me *en gros* and my Lady Stafford in
detail some time before. I will tell you in return, as well as I can,
what happens amongst our acquaintance here. To begin with
family affairs: the Duchess of Kingston grunts on as usual, and I
fear will put us in black bombazine soon, which is a real grief to
me. My dear Aunt Cheyne makes all the money she can of Lady
Frances, and I fear will carry on those politics to the last point,
though the girl is such a fool, 'tis no great matter. I am going
within this half hour to call her to Court.

Our poor cousins the Fieldings are grown yet poorer by the loss of all the little money they had, which in their infinite wisdom they put into the hands of a roguish broker who has fairly walked off with it.

The most diverting story about town at present is in relation to Edgcumbe, though your not knowing the people concerned as well as I do will, I fear, hinder you from being so much entertained by it. I can't tell whether you know a tall, musical, silly, ugly thing, niece to Lady Essex Robartes, who is called Miss Legh. She went a few days ago to visit Mrs. Betty Tichborne, Lady Sunderland's sister, who lives in the house with her, and was denied at the door; but with the true manners of a great fool told the porter that if his lady was at home she was very positive she would be very glad to see her. Upon which she was showed upstairs to Miss Tichborne, who was ready to drop down at the sight of her, and could not help asking her in a grave way how she got in, being denied to every mortal, intending to pass the evening in devout preparations. Miss Legh said she had sent away her chair and servants with intent of staying till nine o'clock. There was then no remedy and she was asked to sit down, but had not been there a quarter of an hour when she heard a violent rap at the door, and somebody vehemently run upstairs. Miss Tichborne seemed much surprised and said she believed it was Mr. Edgcumbe, and was quite amazed how he took it into his head to visit her. During these excuses, enter Edgcumbe, who appeared frighted at the sight of a third person. Miss Tichborne told him almost at his entrance that the lady he saw there was a perfect mistress of music, and as he passionately loved it she thought she could not oblige him more than by desiring her to play. Miss Legh very willingly sat to the harpsichord, upon which her audience decamped to the bedchamber, and left her to play over three or four lessons to herself. They returned, and made what excuses they could, but said very frankly they had not heard her performance and begged her to begin again, which she complied with, and gave them the opportunity of a second retirement. Miss Legh was by this time all fire and flame to see her heavenly harmony thus slighted, and when they returned told them she did not understand playing to an empty room. Mr.

Edgcumbe begged ten thousand pardons, and said if she would play "Gode," it was a tune he died to hear, and it would be an obligation he should never forget. She made answer, she would do him a much greater obligation by her absence, which she supposed was all that was wanting at that time, and ran downstairs in a great fury, to publish as fast as she could, and was so indefatigable in this pious design that in four and twenty hours all the people in town had heard the story, and poor Edgcumbe met with nothing wherever he went but compliments about his third tune, which is reckoned very handsome in a lover past forty.

My Lady Sunderland could not avoid hearing this gallant history, and three days after invited Miss Legh to dinner, where in the presence of her sister and all the servants in waiting, she told her she was very sorry she had been so rudely treated in her house; that it was very true Mr. Edgcumbe had been a perpetual companion of her sister's this two year, and she thought it high time he should explain himself; and she expected her sister should act in this matter as discreetly as Lady K. Pelham had done in the like case, who she heard had given Mr. Pelham four months to resolve in, and after that he was either to marry or lose her for ever. Sir Robert Sutton interrupted her by saying that he never doubted the honor of Mr. Edgcumbe and was persuaded he would have no ill design in his family. The affair stands thus, and Edgcumbe has four months to provide himself elsewhere, during which time he has free egress and regress, and 'tis seriously the opinion of many that a wedding will in good earnest be brought about by this admirable conduct.

I send you a novel instead of a letter, but as it is in your power to shorten it when you please by reading no farther than you like, I will make no excuses for the length of it.

TO LADY BUTE (28 January 1753)

Dear Child,

You have given me a great deal of satisfaction by your account of your eldest daughter. I am particularly pleased to hear she is a good arithmetician; it is the best proof of understanding. The knowledge of numbers is one of the chief distinctions between us and brutes. If there is anything in blood, you may reasonably expect your children should be endowed with an uncommon share of good sense. Mr. Wortley's family and mine have both produced some of [the] greatest men that have been born in England. I mean Admiral Sandwich, and my great-grandfather who was distinguished by the name of Wise William. I have heard Lord Bute's father mentioned as an extraordinary genius (though he had not many opportunities of showing it), and his uncle the present Duke of Argyle has one of the best heads I ever knew.

I will therefore speak to you as supposing Lady Mary not only capable but desirous of learning. In that case, by all means let her be indulged in it. You will tell me, I did not make it a part of your education. Your prospect was very different from hers, as you had no defect either in mind or person to hinder, and much in your circumstances to attract, the highest offers. It seemed your business to learn how to live in the world, as it is hers to know how to be easy out of it. It is the common error of builders and parents to follow some plan they think beautiful (and perhaps is so) without considering that nothing is beautiful that is misplaced. Hence we see so many edifices raised that the raisers can never inhabit, being too large for their fortunes. Vistas are laid open over barren heaths, and apartments contrived for a coolness very agreeable in Italy but killing in the North of Britain. Thus every woman endeavors to breed her daughter a fine lady, qualifying her for a station in which she will never appear, and at the same time incapacitating her for that retirement to which she is destined. Learning (if she has a real taste for it) will not only make her contented but happy in it. No entertainment is so cheap as reading, nor any pleasure so lasting. She will not want new fashions nor regret the loss of expensive diversions or variety of company if she can be amused with an author in her closet. To render this amusement extensive, she should be permitted to learn the languages. I have heard it lamented that boys lose so many years in mere learning of words. This is no objection to a girl, whose time is not so precious. She cannot advance herself in any profession, and has therefore more hours to spare;

and as you say her memory is good, she will be very agreeably employed this way.

There are two cautions to be given on this subject: first, not to think herself learned when she can read Latin or even Greek. Languages are more properly to be called vehicles of learning than learning itself, as may be observed in many schoolmasters, who though perhaps critics in grammar are the most ignorant fellows upon earth. True knowledge consists in knowing things, not words. I would wish her no farther a linguist than to enable her to read books in their originals, that are often corrupted and always injured by translations. Two hours application every morning will bring this about much sooner than you can imagine, and she will have leisure enough beside to run over the English poetry, which is a more important part of a woman's education than it is generally supposed. Many a young damsel has been ruined by a fine copy of verses, which she would have laughed at if she had known it had been stolen from Mr. Waller. I remember when I was a girl I saved one of my companions from destruction, who communicated to me an epistle she was quite charmed with. As she had a natural good taste, she observed the lines were not so smooth as Prior's or Pope's, but had more thought and spirit than any of theirs. She was wonderfully delighted with such a demonstration of her lover's sense and passion, and not a little pleased with her own charms, that had force enough to inspire such elegancies. In the midst of this triumph, I showed her they were taken from Randolph's *Poems*, and the unfortunate transcriber was dismissed with the scorn he deserved. To say truth, the poor plagiary was very unlucky to fall into my hands; that author, being no longer in fashion, would have escaped anyone of less universal reading than myself. You should encourage your daughter to talk over with you what she reads, and as you are very capable of distinguishing, take care she does not mistake pert folly for wit and humour, or rhyme for poetry, which are the common errors of young people, and have a train of ill consequences.

The second caution to be given her (and which is most absolutely necessary) is to conceal whatever learning she attains, with as much solicitude as she would hide crookedness or lameness. The parade of it can only serve to draw on her the envy, and consequently the most inveterate hatred, of all he and she fools, which will certainly be at least three parts in four of all her acquaintance. The use of knowledge in our sex (beside the amusement of solitude) is to moderate the passions and learn to be contented with a small expense, which are the certain effects of a studious life and, it may be, preferable even to that fame which men have engrossed to themselves and will not suffer us to share. You will tell me I have not observed this rule myself, but you are mistaken; it is only inevitable accident that has given me any reputation that way. I have always carefully avoided it, and ever thought it a misfortune.

The explanation of this paragraph would occasion a long digression, which I will not trouble you with, it being my present design only to say what I think useful for the instruction of my granddaughter, which I have much at heart. If she has the same inclination (I should say passion) for learning that I was born with, history, geography, and philosophy will furnish her with materials to pass away cheerfully a longer life than is allotted to mortals. I believe there are few heads capable of making Sir I[saac] Newton's calculations, but the result of them is not difficult to be understood by a moderate capacity. Do not fear this should make her affect the character of Lady ————, or Lady ————, or Mrs. ————. Those women are ridiculous, not because they have learning but because they have it not. One thinks herself a complete historian after reading Echard's *Roman History*, another a profound philosopher having got by heart some of Pope's unintelligible essays, and a third an able divine on the strength of Whitefield's Sermons. Thus you hear them screaming politics and controversy. It is a saying of Thucydides, Ignorance is bold, and knowledge reserved. Indeed it is impossible to be far advanced in it without being more humbled by a conviction of human ignorance than elated by learning.

At the same time I recommend books, I neither exclude work nor drawing. I think it as scandalous for a woman not to know how to use a needle, as for a man not to know how to use a sword. I was once extreme fond of my pencil, and it was a great mortification to me when my father turned off my master, having made a considerable progress for the short time I learnt. My over eagerness in the pursuit of it had brought a weakness on my eyes that made it necessary to leave it off, and all the advantage I got was the improvement of my hand. I see by hers that practise will make her a ready writer. She may attain it by serving you for a secretary when your health or affairs make it troublesome for you to write yourself, and custom will make it an agreeable amusement to her. She cannot have too many for that station of life which will probably be her fate. The ultimate end of your education was to make you a good wife (and I have the comfort to hear that you are one); hers ought to be, to make her happy in a virgin state. I will not say it is happier, but it is undoubtedly safer than any marriage. In a lottery where there are (at the lowest computation) ten thousand blanks to a prize, it is the most prudent choice not to venture.

I have always been so thoroughly persuaded of this truth that notwithstanding the flattering views I had for you, (as I never intended you a sacrifice to my vanity) I thought I owed you the justice to lay before you all the hazards attending matrimony. You may recollect I did so in the strongest manner. Perhaps you may have more success in the instructing your daughter. She has so much company at home she will not need seeking it abroad, and will more readily take the notions you think fit to give her. As you were alone in my family, it would have been thought a great cruelty to suffer you no companions of your own age, especially having so many near relations, and I do not wonder their opinions influenced yours. I was not sorry to see you not determined on a single life, knowing it was not your father's intention, and contented myself with endeavoring to make your home so easy that you might not be in haste to leave it.

I am afraid you will think this a very long and insignificant letter. I hope the kindness of the design will excuse it, being willing to give you every proof in my power that I am your most affectionate mother,

                    M. Wortley.

TO LADY BUTE (6 March 1753)

I cannot help writing a sort of apology for my last letter, foreseeing that you will think it wrong, or at least Lord Bute will be extremely shocked at the proposal of a learned education for daughters, which the generality of men believe as great a profanation as the clergy would do if the laity should presume to exercise the functions of the priesthood. I desire you would take notice I would not have learning enjoined them as a task, but permitted as a pleasure if their genius leads them naturally to it. I look upon my granddaughters as a sort of lay nuns. Destiny may have laid up other things for them, but they have no reason to expect to pass their time otherwise than their aunts do at present, and I know by experience it is in the power of study not only to make solitude tolerable but agreeable. I have now lived almost seven years in a stricter retirement than yours in the Isle of Bute, and can assure you I have never had half an hour heavy on my hands for want of something to do.

Whoever will cultivate their own mind will find full employment. Every virtue does not only require great care in the planting, but as much daily solicitude in cherishing as exotic fruits and flowers; the vices and passions (which I am afraid are the natural product of the soil) demand perpetual weeding. Add to this the search after knowledge (every branch of which is entertaining), and the longest life is too short for the pursuit of it, which, though in some regards confined to very strait limits, leaves still a vast variety of amusements to those capable of tasting them, which is utterly impossible for those that are blinded by prejudices, which are the certain effect of an ignorant education. My own was one of the worst in the world, being exactly the same as Clarissa Harlowe's, her pious Mrs. Norton so perfectly resembling my governess (who had been nurse to my mother) I could almost fancy the author was acquainted with her. She took so much pains from my infancy to fill my head with superstitious tales and false notions, it was none of her fault I am not at this day afraid of witches and hobgoblins, or turned Methodist.

Almost all girls are bred after this manner. I believe you are the only woman (perhaps I might say person) that never was either frighted or cheated into anything by your parents. I can truly affirm I never deceived anybody in my life excepting (which I confess has often happened undesignedly) by speaking plainly. As Earl Stanhope used to say (during his ministry), he always imposed on the Foreign Ministers by telling them the naked truth, which as they thought impossible to come from the mouth of a statesman, they never failed to write informations to their respective courts directly contrary to the assurances he gave them, most people confounding the ideas of sense and cunning, though there are really no two things in nature more opposite. It is in part from this false reasoning, the unjust custom prevails of debarring our sex from the advantages of learning, the men fancying the improvement of our understandings would only furnish us with more art to deceive them, which is directly contrary to the truth. Fools are always enterprising, not seeing the difficulties of deceit or the ill consequences of detection. I could give many examples of ladies whose ill conduct has been very notorious, which has been owing to that ignorance which has exposed them to idleness, which is justly called the mother of mischief.

There is nothing so like the education of a woman of quality as that of a prince. They are taught to dance and the exterior part of what is called good breeding, which if they attain they are extraordinary creatures in their kind, and have all the accomplishments required by their directors. The same characters are formed by the same lessons, which inclines me to think (if I dare say it) that Nature has not placed us in an inferior rank to men, no more than the females of other animals, where we see no distinction of capacity, though I am persuaded if there was a commonwealth of rational horses (as Doctor Swift has supposed) it would be an established maxim amongst them that a mare could not be taught to pace. I could add a great deal on this subject, but I am not now endeavoring to remove the prejudices of mankind. My only design is to point out to my granddaughters the method of being contented with that retreat to which probably their circumstances will oblige them, and which is perhaps preferable to all the show of public life. It has always been my inclination. Lady Stafford (who knew me better than anybody else in the world, both from her own just discernment, and my heart being ever as open to her as myself) used to tell me my true vocation was a monastery, and I now find by experience more sincere pleasures with my books and garden than all the flutter of a court could give me.

If you follow my advice in relation to Lady Mary, my correspondence may be of use to her, and I shall very willingly give her those instructions that may be necessary in the pursuit of her studies. Before her age I was in the most regular commerce with my grandmother, though the difference of our time of life was much greater, she being past forty-five when she married my grandfather. She died at ninety-six, retaining to the last the vivacity and clearness of her understanding, which was very uncommon. You cannot remember her, being then in your nurse's arms. I conclude with repeating to you, I only recommend, but am far from commanding, which I think I have no right to do. I tell you my sentiments because you desired to know them, and hope you will receive them with some partiality as coming from your most affectionate mother,

M. Wortley.

TO LADY BUTE (23 July 1754)

My Dear Child,

I have promised you some remarks on all the books I have received. I believe you would easily forgive my not keeping my word; however, I shall go on. The Rambler is certainly a strong misnomer. He always plods in the beaten road of his predecessors, following the Spectator (with the same pace a pack horse would do a hunter) in the style that is proper to lengthen a paper. These writers may perhaps be of service to the public (which is saying a great deal in their favor). There are numbers of both sexes who never read anything but such productions, and cannot spare time from doing nothing to go through a sixpenny pamphlet. Such gentle readers may be improved by a moral hint which, though repeated over and over from generation to generation, they never heard in their lives. I should be glad to know the name of this laborious author.

H[enry] Fielding has given a true picture of himself and his first wife in the characters of Mr. and Mrs. Booth (some compliment to his own figure excepted) and I am persuaded several of the incidents he mentions are real matters of fact. I wonder he does not perceive Tom Jones and Mr. Booth are sorry scoundrels. All these sort of books have the same fault, which I cannot easily pardon, being very mischievous. They place a merit in extravagant passions, and encourage young people to hope for impossible events to draw them out of the misery they choose to plunge themselves into, expecting legacies from unknown relations, and generous benefactors to distressed virtue, as much out of nature as fairy treasures. Fielding has really a fund of true humour, and was to be pitied at his first entrance into the world, having no choice (as he said himself) but to be a hackney writer or a hackney coachman. His genius deserved a better fate, but I cannot help blaming that continued indiscretion (to give it the softest name) that has run through his life, and I am afraid still remains. I guessed R[oderick] Random to be his, though without his name. I cannot think [Ferdinand Count] Fathom wrote by the same hand; it is every way so much below it.

Sally [Fielding] has mended her style in her last volume of D[avid] Simple, which conveys a useful moral (though she does not seem to have intended it); I mean, shows the ill consequences of not providing against casual losses, which happen to almost everybody. Mrs. Orgueil's character is well drawn, and is frequently to be met with. The *Art of Tormenting,* the *Female Quixote,* and *Sir C[harles] Goodville* are all sale work. I suppose they proceed from her pen, and heartily pity her, constrained by her circumstances to seek her bread by a method I do not doubt she despises. Tell me who is that accomplished countess she celebrates. I left no such person in London; nor can I imagine who is meant by the English Sappho mentioned in *Betsy Thoughtless,* whose adventures, and those of Jenny Jessamy, gave me some amusement. I was better entertained by the *Valet,* who very fairly represents how you are bought and sold by your servants. I am now so accustomed to another manner of treatment, it would be difficult for me to suffer them. His adventures have the uncommon merit of ending in a surprising manner.

The general want of invention which reigns amongst our writers inclines me to think it is not the natural growth of our island, which has not sun enough to warm the imagination; the press is loaded by the servile flock of imitators. (Lord B[olingbroke] would have quoted Horace in this place.) Since I was born, no original has appeared excepting Congreve, and Fielding, who would I believe have approached nearer to his excellencies if not forced by necessity to publish without correction, and throw many productions into the world he would have thrown into the fire if meat could have been got without money, or money without scribbling. The greatest virtue, justice, and the most distinguishing prerogative of mankind, writing, when duly executed do honor to human nature, but when degenerated into trades are the most contemptible ways of getting bread. I am sorry not to see any more of P[eregrine] Pickle's performances; I wish you would tell me his name.

I can't forbear saying something in relation to my granddaughters, who are very near my heart. If any of them are fond of reading, I would not advise you to hinder them (chiefly because it is impossible) seeing poetry, plays or romances; but accustom them to talk over what they read, and point to them, as you are very capable of doing, the absurdity often concealed under fine expressions, where the sound is apt to engage the admiration of young people. I was so much charmed at fourteen with the Dialogue of Henry and Emma, I can say it by heart to this day, without reflecting on the monstrous folly of the story in plain prose, where a young heiress to a fond father is represented falling in love with a fellow she had only seen as a huntsman, a falconer, and a beggar, and who confesses, without any circumstances of excuse, that he is obliged to run his country, having newly committed a murder. She ought reasonably to have supposed him (at best) a highwayman, yet the virtuous virgin resolves to run away with him to live amongst the banditti, and wait upon his trollop if she had no other way of enjoying his company. This senseless tale is, however, so well varnished with melody of words and pomp of sentiments, I am convinced it has hurt more girls than ever were injured by the lewdest poems extant.

I fear this counsel has been repeated to you before, but I

have lost so many letters designed for you, I know not which you have received. If you would have me avoid this fault, you must take notice of those that arrive, which you very seldom do.

My dear child, God bless you and yours. I am ever your most affectionate mother,

M. Wortley.

Notes

LETTER TO PHILIPPA MUNDY (10 January 1713)
Years later, Montagu boasted that she and Wortley had lived on less than £800 during the first year of their marriage. (*Halsband*)
The two quotations (slightly garbled) are from Matthew Prior's "Henry and Emma," lines 378–82 and 310–11, on which see her comments in her letter to her daughter of 23 July 1754. Emma's love was imprudent to the point of folly, but it turned out well in the end.

LETTER TO LADY_____ (1 April 1717)
"glasses"—glass windows
"the majestic grace which Milton describes"—see the introductory description of Eve in *Paradise Lost, IV,* 304–18. (*Halsband*)
"Mr. Jervas"—Charles Jervas, a fashionable portrait painter who had painted Montagu in 1710   (*Halsband*)
"stays"—the long, stiff corset of the period

LETTER TO THE COUNTESS OF_____ (May 1718)
The letter goes on to describe the religious and marital customs of the Armenians.
"ferigé"—Turkish women were not "permitted to go into the streets without two muslins; one that covers her face all but her eyes, and another that hides the whole dress of her head, and hangs halfway down her back, and their shapes are wholly concealed by a thing they called a ferigé . . . this has strait sleeves, that reach to their finger-ends, and it laps all round them, not unlike a riding-hood" (letter to the Countess of Mar, April, 1717).

Montagu did in fact use as sources Richard Knolles's history of the Turks and its continuation by Paul Rycaut (completed 1700). *(Halsband)*
Lucretia, raped by Sextus, committed suicide.
"following our name"—willing our property to a person bearing our name, however distant a relative.

LETTER TO LADY MAR (23 June 1727)
Lady Frances Pierrepont, daughter of Lady Mary's dead brother, brought with her an allowance of £400 a year, and therefore "awakened the consciences of half her relations to take care of her education" (letter to Lady Mar, c. 15 July 1726).
"Gode"—the aria "Gode l'alma" in Handel's opera *Ottone* (revived in 1727) *(Halsband)*
Henry Pelham, possibly Lady Catherine Manners' lover three years earlier, finally married her in 1726; but Edgcumbe, a widower at this time, never remarried. *(Halsband)*

LETTER TO LADY BUTE (28 January 1753)
"the languages"—Latin and Greek, part of every gentleman's education but generally considered unsuitable for women
Thomas Randolph's *Poems* were published in 1638. *(Halsband)*
Laurence Echard's history, Pope's philosophical poems, and George Whitefield's emotional sermons would not satisfy genuine scholars.
"work"—needlework
"hand"—handwriting

LETTER TO LADY BUTE (6 March 1753)
Lord Bute's four sisters were married, but apparently lived in the country. Because of their limited means, Lord and Lady Bute lived on the remote Scottish island of Bute for ten years after their marriage in 1736. *(Halsband)*
Mrs. Norton in Samuel Richardson's *Clarissa* has raised the heroine to be conventionally good, though Richardson did not represent her as superstitious.
James, Earl Stanhope, Secretary of State from 1714 to 1721, was noted for his frank manner. *(Halsband)*
Jonathan Swift imagined "a commonwealth of rational horses" in Book IV of *Gulliver's Travels*.
In a letter to Lady Bute of 20 October 1755, Montagu praised the hero's project of an English Monastery in Samuel Richardson's *Sir*

Charles Grandison: "It was a favorite scheme of mine when I was fifteen, and had I then been mistress of an independent fortune, would certainly have executed it and elected myself Lady Abbess."

LETTER TO LADY BUTE (23 July 1754)
The major works Montagu discusses are Samuel Johnson's *Rambler* (1750–52), a less lively work than the *Spectator* of Joseph Addison and Richard Steele (1711–12), but one having a dignified wisdom that she does not recognize; Henry Fielding's *Amelia* (1751), which centers on the Booths, and *Tom Jones* (1749), both of which have implausibly happy endings; Tobias Smollett's *Roderick Random* (1748), *Ferdinand Count Fathom* (1753), and *Peregrine Pickle* (1751); and Sarah Fielding's *David Simple* (1744), which ends with a series of misfortunes. Her Mrs. Orgueil is a hypocritical villain. The other works are Jane Collier's *An Essay on the Art of Ingeniously Tormenting* (1753); Charlotte Lennox's *The Female Quixote* (1752), where a wise, kindly countess helps to educate the heroine; Eliza Haywood's *History of Miss Betsy Thoughtless* (1751) and *History of Jemmy and Jenny Jessamy* (1753); and the anonymous *Memoirs of Sir Charles Goodville* (1753) and *Adventures of a Valet* (1752). Her derisive plot summary of Matthew Prior's poem "Henry and Emma" is accurate.

Despite her disparaging comment, Montagu greatly admired *Tom Jones*, writing "Ne plus ultra" (the highest point of perfection) in her personal copy. Henry and Sarah Fielding were cousins of hers.

The relevant Horatian quotation is "O imitatores, servum pecus . . ." (*Epistles* I. xix. 19).   (*Halsband*)

Bibliographical Note

The Letters and Works of Lady Mary Wortley Montagu, edited by her great grandson Lord J. S. W. Wharncliffe, were published in 1837. Robert Halsband has edited the definitive edition of her *Complete Letters* (Oxford: Clarendon, 1965), as well as *The Nonsense of Common-Sense* (Evanston: Northwestern University, 1947) and, with Isobel Grundy, the *Essays and Poems of Lady Mary Wortley Montagu* (New York: Oxford University Press, 1977).

Halsband has also written the definitive biography, *The Life of Lady Mary Wortley Montagu* (Oxford: Clarendon, 1956).

CHARLOTTE SMITH

Charlotte Turner (1749–1806), daughter of a landed gentleman, received the customary education of a young lady. Her father's decision to remarry (her mother having died when she was three) precipitated her own marriage, though she was only fifteen. The young man, Benjamin Smith, was the son and business partner of a wealthy merchant. The marriage was disastrous, as Smith proved to be inconsiderate and irresponsible. (He appears as the impossible Mr. Stafford in Charlotte's first novel and in many of her subsequent works.) Benjamin's father died in 1776, leaving a large inheritance to his grandchildren; but unfortunately they could not profit from it, since his complicated will caused thirty years of litigation. It was Charlotte of course who had to struggle with the lawyers; she expressed her fury through her recurrent characters of dishonest, dilatory lawyers who treat women with contempt.

Benjamin Smith was imprisoned for debt in 1783, and, while she was staying with him in prison, she thought of making money by her poems. Her *Elegiac Sonnets* (1784) were an immediate success. But, though she preferred poetry, she turned to novel-writing as more lucrative. After twenty-three years of marriage and twelve children, she decided she had to leave her husband, and she became a professional writer. *Emmeline* (1788), her first novel, was enthusiastically received. For the next ten years, she produced an average of one four-volume novel per year. Though she was successful, generally receiving £50 per volume, she wrote under relentless financial pressure; for she had her nine surviving children to support and establish in the world.

It is not surprising, then, that her novels suffer from padding and hasty construction. Only occasionally was she sufficiently free from care to write to her full potential, as in the first part of her best novel, *The Old Manor House* (1793). Writing to support herself, she had to satisfy her readers' demands for unreal sentimental romance such as Mrs. Denzil satirizes in *The Banished Man* (1794). Nevertheless, she was not afraid to advocate opinions considered unseemly in a lady novelist. She presented a relatively liberal attitude toward sexual morality, and, at a time when women were not expected to express political views of any kind, she did not hesitate to denounce British policy during the American Revolution in *The Old Manor House* and to defend the French Revolution in *Desmond* (1792). She does not, however, appear to have been particularly feminist: her insistence that she wrote from financial necessity suggests that she would have preferred to lead the sheltered life of a conventional eighteenth-century lady.

FROM *DESMOND*

In *Desmond*, Charlotte Smith shocked her readers by representing her virtuous hero in love with an unhappily married woman, Geraldine Verney, and by presenting a sympathetic view of the French Revolution, which had abolished the special privileges of the nobility and the clergy, but had not yet reached the excesses of the Reign of Terror. She set up numerous conversations, too long to reproduce here, in which characters opposing the Revolution expose their self-interest and unthinking complacency. In her Preface, she defended herself against both criticisms.

In representing a young man nourishing an ardent but concealed passion for a married woman, I certainly do not mean to encourage or justify such attachments; but no delineation of character appears to me more interesting than that of a man capable of such a passion so generous and disinterested as to seek only the good of its object, nor any story more moral than one that represents the existence of an affection so regulated.

As to the political passages dispersed through the work, they are, for the most part, drawn from conversations to which I have been a witness, in England and France, during the last twelve months. In carrying on my story in those countries, and at a period when their political situation (but particularly that of the latter) is the general topic of discourse in both, I have given to my imaginary characters the arguments I have heard on both sides; and if those in favor of one party have evidently the advantage, it is not owing to my partial representation, but to the predominant power of truth and reason, which can neither be altered nor concealed.

But women it is said have no business with politics—Why not?—Have they no interest in the scenes that are acting around them, in which they have fathers, brothers, husbands, sons, or friends engaged?—Even in the commonest course of female education, they are expected to acquire some knowledge of history; and yet, if they are to have no opinion of what *is* passing, it avails little that they should be informed of what *has passed*, in a world where they are subject to such mental degradation; where they are censured as affecting masculine knowledge if they happen to have any understanding, or despised as insignificant triflers if they have none.

Knowledge which qualifies women to speak or to write on any other than the most common and trivial subjects is supposed to be of so difficult attainment, that it cannot be acquired but by the sacrifice of domestic virtues or the neglect of domestic duties. —*I* however may safely say, that it was in the *observance*, not in the *breach* of duty, *I* became an Author; and it has happened that the circumstances which have compelled me to write, have introduced me to those scenes of life and those varieties of character which I should otherwise never have seen: Though alas! it is from thence that I am too well enabled to describe from *immediate* observation,

> The proud man's contumely, th'oppressor's wrong;
> The law's delay, the insolence of office.

But, while in consequence of the affairs of my family, being most unhappily in the power of men who *seem to exercise all these with impunity*, I am become an *Author by profession*, and feel every year more acutely *"that hope delayed maketh the heart sick."* I am sensible also (to use another quotation) that

> _____ Adversity—
> Though like a toad ugly and venomous,
> Wears yet a precious jewel in its head.

For it is to my involuntary appearance in that character that I am indebted for all that makes my continuance in the world desirable, all that softens the rigor of my destiny and enables me to sustain it: I mean friends among those, who, while their talents are the boast of their country, are yet more respectable for the goodness and integrity of their hearts.

Among these I include a female friend, to whom I owe the beautiful little Ode in the last volume, who having written it for this work, allows me thus publicly to boast of a friendship which is the pride and pleasure of my life.

If I may be indulged a moment longer in my egotism, it shall be only while I apologize for the typographical errors of the work, which may have been in some measure occasioned by the detached and hurried way in which the sheets were sometimes sent to the press when I was at a distance from it, and when my attention was distracted by the troubles which it seems to be the peculiar delight of the persons who are concerned in the management of my children's affairs to inflict upon me. With all this the public have nothing to do: but were it proper to relate all the disadvantages from anxiety of mind and local circumstances under which these volumes have been composed, such a detail might be admitted as an excuse for more material errors.

For that asperity of remark, which will arise on the part of those whose political tenets I may offend, I am prepared; those who object to the matter, will probably arraign the manner, and exclaim against the impropriety of making a book of entertainment the vehicle of political discussion. I am however conscious that in making these slight sketches of manners and opinions, as they fluctuated around me, I have not sacrificed truth to any party—Nothing appears to me more respectable than national pride; nothing so absurd as national prejudice—And in the faithful representation of the manners of other countries, surely Englishmen may find abundant reason to indulge the one, while they conquer the other. To those however who still cherish the idea of our having a *natural* enemy in the French nation, and that they are still more *naturally* our foes because they have dared to be freemen, I can only say that against the phalanx of prejudice kept in constant pay and under strict discipline by interest, the slight skirmishing of a novel writer can have no effect: we see it remains hitherto unbroken against the powerful efforts of learning and genius—though united in that cause which *must* finally triumph —the cause of truth, reason, and humanity.

The heroine's lively unmarried sister, Fanny Waverly, writing to Geraldine, describes the limitations of her life under the supervision of their narrow-minded, conventional mother:

Now do I long to tell you a little of what is passing here, but I know the gossip of this place is rather irksome than pleasing to you; and I am often rather reproved than thanked for endeavoring to amuse you with the events, real or imaginary, which occupy us here, and give us the requisite supplies of conversation for the tea and card parties; but, indeed, my Geraldine, if you deprive me by your rigid aversion to what you call detraction of such a resource, I know not what there will remain for me to write about and to fill those long letters which alone satisfy you; I must not say much of any of our own family, because you say it is pert, and undutiful, and I know not what; if I could repeat only good of the people I am among, you would let me fill quires of paper about them; but, as it is, if I report only what I hear, you accuse me of being as spitefully scandalous as the dowagers, who sit in tremendous committees on the reputations of the week —You know, I never am allowed to converse with any of the literary people I meet, as my mother has a terrible aversion to everything that looks like a desire to acquire knowledge; and for the same reason, she proscribes every species of reading, and murmurs when she cannot absolutely prohibit the fashionable, insipid novel.

There is so much enquiry of the sage, matronly gentlewomen of her acquaintance, who are, as she believes, deep in the secret, as to *what* books are proper, who are the authors, and whether there be "any offence in them," that, by the time these voices are collected, I find more than half I propose reading absolutely forbidden—Novels, it is decided, convey the poison of bad example in the soft semblance of a refined sentiment—One contains an oblique apology for suicide; a second, a lurking palliation of conjugal infidelity; a third, a sneer against parental authority; and a fourth, against religion; some are disliked for doctrines which probably malice only, assuming the garb of wisdom, can discover in them; and others, because their writers have, either in their private or political life, given offence to the prudery or the party of some of these worthy personages whom my mother, relying on their reputation for sanctity and sagacity, chooses to consult; and thus I am reduced to practise the *finesse* of a boarding-school miss, and to hide these objectionable pages from an inquisition not less severe than that which the lovely Serena sustained; or I must confine myself to such mawkish reading as is produced "in a rivulet of text running through a meadow of margin," in the soft semblance of letters "from Miss Everilda Evelyn, to Miss Victoria Villars"—How then, my sister, am I to find anything to say but of living characters? or how can I help being satirical against those who will not let me be sentimental?—I might, indeed, read history; but whenever I attempt to do so, I am, to tell you the truth, driven from it by disgust—What is it but a miserably mortifying detail of crimes and follies?—of the guilt of a few and the sufferings of many, while almost every page offers an argument in favor of what I never will believe—that heaven created the human race only to destroy itself; and that in placing the various species of it in various climates, whence they acquired various complexions, habits, and languages, their Creator meant these men should become the natural enemies of each other, and apply the various portions of reason he has allotted them only in studying how to annoy and murder each other.

But I am wandering, in my wild way, from the point; and, in my complaints that the pretty, soothing tales of imagination are prohibited, while the hideous realities of human life affright me, I had nearly forgotten what I was going to say, which is not at all scandalous—Oh no!—it is, on the contrary, an event at which you will rejoice—Your old friend, Miss Elford, has, at last, met with a lover, who really purposes to become her husband— He is a physician; very well looking, and twelve or fourteen years younger than herself—She is in love!—Oh! undescribably in love —And the Doctor foresees, in her extensive connections, advantages likely to arise to him in his profession, that will, he thinks, more than counterbalance the trifling wants of fortune, beauty, and youth. . . . The idea here is that they are to be married very soon, and I really wish they may, if it be only in the hope that Miss Elford, in having a husband of her own, will be so engaged by her own unexpected good fortune as to let the rest of the world remain for some time unmolested. I cannot help it, my dear sister, if, in despite of your gentle admonitions, I do hate this little, shrivelled, satirical sybil. . . . Oh! if you should have heard how she canted about "her dear, her amiable Mrs. Verney," while she could not disguise the pleasure she took in describing your husband's foibles—you would have been convinced of what I always told you, that under uncommon hypocrisy, she conceals uncommon malignity—As to myself, I find she goes about talking of me in such terms as these: "Did you see dear Miss Waverly at the ball last night?—Was she not charming?—I think she never looked so well; and really I begin to be a convert to the opinion of those who said last year, when she first came out, that she was quite as handsome as her second sister, Mrs. Verney, the celebrated beauty—Mrs. Verney, poor, dear creature!—(I have an amazing regard for her, and have loved her from our *childhood*, though she is two or three years younger than I am!) Mrs. Verney is a little altered, though still so very young—Poor thing! —troubles, like hers, are great enemies to beauty, which is but as the flower of the morning; but however she may be changed in appearance, she is still most amiable—indeed, more so, as to gentleness of temper, than Miss Waverly, though *she* is a sweet girl, and has no fault, except, perhaps, a little, a very little too much vivacity, which it is the great object of my worthy friend, her mother, to check; judging, indeed, very truly, that a young person, so much followed and admired, cannot be too reserved and cautious."—Yes! and, in consequence of this impertinent opinion, this odious tabby (who says she is only a year or two younger than you, though she will never see forty again) has made my mother so full of fears and precautions, that I am neither to read any books but those that are ordered by the Divan, of which she is deputy chairwoman, or to speak to any men but old fograms, such as Major Danby; or men of large fortune—My mother need not be so apprehensive; first, because I have not the least inclination to set out for Scotland with any of the insignificant butterflies, whom I like well enough to have flutter about me in public; and secondly, because, if I had such a fancy, there is not one of them who has the least notion of marrying a young woman without a fortune, or with a very small one—Even the fortunate beings who are not proscribed, men who can make a settlement, have, for the most part, but little inclination to encumber themselves with a portionless wife; and among them all, I know none who answer my ideas of what a man ought to be

—Alas there is but one in the world whom I should select as the hero of my Romance, if I were in haste to make one.

In one of the numerous political discussions in the novel, Desmond, the virtuous and thoughtful hero, argues that the political system of England could be improved:

I would have our boast of [our country's] excellence just—I would not have it the mere cant which we have learned by rote, and repeat by habit; though, when we venture to think about it, we know that it is vanity and prejudice, and not truth, when we speak of its wonderful perfection; and that even those who are its most decided partisans are continually betrayed into an acknowledgement of its defects.—Boswell, in his life of Johnson says that "in the British parliament, any question, however unreasonable or unjust, may be carried by a venal majority."—This is acknowledged truth; and it follows that, while the means of corruption exist to an extent so immense, there must be a venal majority; and, of course, every question, however ruinous, will be carried. —While this is the case, and while every attempt to remedy this *original sin* of the constitution is opposed (though the necessity of that remedy has been allowed by the greatest statesmen of our country), while every proposal to make it *really* what it is only *nominally* raises a cry as if the subversion of the whole empire was intended—I cannot agree to unlimited praise—and, though most certainly willing to allow to you that a greater portion of happiness is diffused among the subjects of the British government than among any other people upon earth; but this rather proves that their condition is very wretched, than that ours is perfectly happy.—Carried on a little in the same way, was the argument that I heard not long since, *against* the abolition of the detestable Slave Trade—I was pleading *for it* with a *member of parliament, who has an estate in the West Indies,* and who has been there himself, some years ago, when he commanded a man of war—I talked warmly (for I had just been reading the reports of the committee) and I talked from my heart.—My adversary, well hackneyed in the ways of men, treated all I could say as the ill-digested speculation of a hot-head enthusiast, who knew nothing of the matter.—"You are young, Mr. Desmond," said he, "very young, and have but little considered the importance of this trade to the prosperity of the British nation; besides, give me leave to tell you, that you know nothing of the condition of the negroes neither, nor of their nature—They are not fit to be treated otherwise than as slaves, for they have not the same senses and feeling as we have—A negro fellow minds a flogging so little, that he will go to a dance at night, or at least the next day, after a hearty application of the cat—They have no understanding to qualify them for any rank in society above slaves; and, indeed, are not to be called men—they are monkeys."—"Monkeys! Sir!" exclaimed I, "that is, indeed, a most extraordinary assertion.—Monkeys! I believe, indeed, they are a very distinct race from the European—So also is the straight-haired and fine formed Asiatic —So are the red men of North America—But where, amid this variety, does the man end, and the monkey begin? I am afraid if we follow whither this enquiry will lead us, that we shall find ourselves more degraded than even by the whimsical system of Lord Monboddo.—If the negro, however, is a monkey, let me hazard one remark—that their very near affinity to us is too clearly ascertained by the alliances we have formed with them; nay, I have even heard that captains of our ships of war have often professed that they prefer the sable nymphs of Africa to the fairer dames of Europe—'The pale unripen'd beauties of the North.'

And, if I recollect aright, Sir, I have formerly, in moments of unguarded conviviality, heard you say that when you were a young man, and in the sea service, you had yourself indulged this partiality for these monkey ladies."

This parried, a little, the round assertion that negroes were not men; but he still insisted upon it that they had little or no feeling; it was not, however, very difficult to prove, as far as proof can on such a point be brought, that their physical and moral sensibility is more acute than ours.—I will not lengthen my letter by repeating these proofs, because I am persuaded you are not disposed to dispute them; but go on to say that after I had carried almost every article against him, my adversary was compelled to take shelter under such an argument as yours.—"Perhaps," said he, "the negroes *are* sometimes beat, but not half so much as our soldiers are—The punishment inflicted on soldiers is infinitely more severe."

"Does not that, Sir," said I, "rather prove that our military punishments are inhuman, than that the negroes have nothing to complain of?"

Thus, my dear Bethel, it seems to me, that instead of proving that we are extremely happy, you prove only that we are compar· atively so; and, for my part, I never could, as many people do, derive consolation from the reflection that the existence of evil in the person of another diminished the sense of what I felt in my own.

Do not, however, misunderstand me; I think that our form of government is certainly the best—not that can be imagined—but that has ever been experienced; and, while we are sure that practice is in its favor, it would be most absurd to dream of destroying it on theory.—If I had a very good house that had some inconveniences about it, I should not desire to pull it down, but I certainly should send for an architect and say, alter this room—it is too dark—remove those passages—they are too intricate—make a door here, and a staircase there; make the kitchen more habitable for my servants, and then my house will be extremely good—But I should be very much startled if my architect was to say, "Sir, I dare not touch your house—if I let in more light, if I take down those partitions and make the other changes you desire, I am very much afraid that the great timbers will give way, and the *party-walls* crush you beneath their ruins."

FROM *THE BANISHED MAN*

Mrs. Denzil, a woman author modeled on Charlotte Smith herself, describes her way of life in a letter to a sympathetic friend.

I do not pretend to be without faults—and as a poet, I might plead imprudence by prescription. Alas! dear *****, how little can the generality of the prosperous world judge of a situation so unlike their own.—Many of my *ci-devant* friends, for many I have dropped by the way (I beg pardon, they have dropped me), were born to the same prospects of easy competence as I was; and their subsequent destiny—ah! how unlike mine—has *not* belied the early promise of affluence.—These ladies have always had a father, an husband, or a brother, to order all their pecuniary concerns.—The morning arose only to awaken them to some pleasurable party abroad, or some chosen amusement at home—Their winters have passed, and, for aught I know, pass still while they are in London, in shopping or visiting in a morning—or by such as are literary, or are told they ought to be so, in examining new pamphlets, peeping into reviews to form their opinions, listening to that of "Dear Mr. Such-a-one, the most charming man in the world, who writes sweet verses himself"; in entering some *delightful* lines into a book, or following a celebrated preacher, or attending philosophical lectures.—Others, of less mental accomplishments, frequent auctions or exhibitions, or drive into the Park, or walk in Kensington Gardens. The former set (the literary ladies) return to dress for a late dinner, then go to some conversation, where there is "The feast of reason, and the flow of soul," or by their interest with some favourite actress they get places when others are refused, and from their severer studies unbend at a celebrated performance.—The less enlightened, the beauties, or rather those who insist upon being still noticed as such, dress with more éclat, though not with more care—They dash at new fashions to leave the *vulgars and raffs* at an immeasurable distance—dine at eight o'clock—go to the opera; sit up half the night at deep play—talk loud about it the next day as they stop in Bond Street to some idle man who affects fashion. If they happen to be women whose connections were originally in the city, they take care to talk a great deal to and of lords and ladies, Sir John and Sir Frederick, and to exceed in their follies and their expences these new acquaintances.—Such are the lives persons lead, who "are very sorry for poor Mrs. Denzil, but cannot help saying they think her quite wrong in many things— to be sure she has some talents, but nothing so extraordinary; and if she had, it is a thousand pities to use them in attacking people of consequence, who really wished her well—and then to have any opinion of politics is so extremely wrong!—There can be but one opinion on those things among 'les gens comme il faut'—why then offend them by differing from them, when *they* only can be of use in promoting the interest of her large family." —Such are the charitable comments on the conduct of "poor Mrs. Denzil," who leaves her bed in a morning, when her health permits, to go to her desk, from whence she rises only to sit down to a dinner she cannot eat, waited upon by an awkward boy or a strapping country girl, who stare at madam "bin as how she writes all them there books that be on the shelf." From this delectable repast, during which the authoress "Chews the food of sweet and bitter fancy," rather than anything else, she is not unfrequently called on by an honest gentleman in a brown rough great coat, corduroy breeches, boots, and green boot garters, his hair curling naturally in his poll to the great advantage of his shining face, who, with that sort of half bow which a substantial tradesman sometimes makes, as much as to say, "Humph! for all you are a lady, I know you are poor and in debt"—pulls out a little square wafered letter, of which the contents peradventure run thus—

Mrs. Denzil

Madam,

My neighbour, Mr. Thomas Tough, coming your way, I have desired him to call to receive of you the sum of sixty-two pounds, nine shillings and elevenpence, due as per bill delivered for your young gentlemen, I having sent up the same, as desired, to Messieurs Ramsay and Shrimpshire, who answer they have no effects in hand for discharge of ditto;—wherefore hope you will please immediately to pay the same to bearer, whose receipt will be sufficient for,

Madam,
Your humble servant,
Humphry Hotgoose

N.B. Madam, I hope you'll not fail herein, as I have a great sum to make up nixt Wensday, and hope you'll give me no furder trubble; but if should, must put it into a lawyer's hands.

From the tete-à-tete with Mr. Thomas Tough, she goes to her desk again, and begins to write "With what appetite she may,"in the forlorn hope of procuring from her bookseller part of the money she has been compelled to promise to the said Thomas's peremptory demands on behalf of Mr. Humphry Hotgoose—precious recipe to animate the imagination and exalt the fancy!

The evening comes, however, and finds her so employed. After a conference with Mr. Tough, she must write a tender dialogue between some damsel, whose perfections are even greater than those "Which youthful poets fancy when they love," and her hero, who, to the bravery and talents of Caesar, adds the gentleness of Sir Charles Grandison and the wit of Lovelace. But Mr. Tough's conversation, his rude threats, and his boisterous remonstrances have totally sunk her spirits; nor are they elevated by hearing that the small beer is almost out; that the pigs of a rich farmer, her next neighbour, have broke into the garden, rooted up the whole crop of peas, and not left her a single hyacinth or jonquil. She knows remonstrance to be vain; or if it were not, that farmer Duckbury cannot restore her bed of sweet flowers, on which she depended for the amusement of a few solitary moments in the spring. Melancholy and dejected, she recollects that once she had a walled garden well provided with flowers; and the comforts and pleasures of affluence recur forcibly to her mind. She is diverted from such reflections, however, by hearing from her maid, as she is assisting her to undress, that John Gubbins's children over the way, and his wife, and John his-self, have all got the *scarlot favor;* and that one of the children is dead on't, and another like to die. She is ashamed of the concern she felt a few moments before for a nosegay, when creatures of the same species, and so near her, are suffering under calamities infinitely more severe. She enquires what attendants these poor people have had; and finds that farmer Duckbury has sent the doctor (hired by the parish to attend the poor at so much a head), and that he says the favor's very catching, and he's

afraid to go nist um. Compassion for these unhappy persons is
now mingled with apprehensions for her own family. A malig-
nant fever raging in a dirty cottage not an hundred yards from
her door gives her but an unpleasing impression to carry to her
pillow, where "The churlish chiding of the winter's wind" does
not lull her agitated mind to repose. Sleep flies from her eyes; or
if it visits her a moment, the figure of that animal, "Hateful to
gods and men," A Dun, appears before her disturbed imagination; or she sees her sick neighbours expiring around her. With
the earliest dawn she sends her servant (her nose well stopped
with rue) to enquire at their door how they do?—The scene of
exquisite misery, even as described by the unadorned account of
her maid Betty, excites her commiseration. She buys her wine by
the dozen, not having been for a long time rich enough to pur-
chase a pipe, and she sends a man and horse ten miles to fetch it;
but all she has in the house is now sent to supply the pressing
occasions of John Gubbins and his family, for whom she knows it
will do more than medicine, especially such as is sent in to be
paid for by farmer Duckbury, as overseer, at so much a head. The
rest of the day is passed as before; her hero and her heroine are
parted in agonies, or meet in delight, and she is employed in
making the most of either; with interludes of the Gubbins family,
and precautions against importing the infectious distemper into
her own. The farmer arrives towards evening, who had been to
the market-town and had undertaken to bring her letters. He
delivers her two, of which the contents are probably as follows:

No. 4, Thavies Inn, Feb. 28, 17—

Madam,

The trustees have received yours of the 9th past. I hereby
acquaint you from them, that they will not, for the future, corre-
spond with you, or answer any questions you may ask. They are
surprised at the abuse you throw upon them about Mr. Pretty-
thief, their agent. You have already been informed that the
trustees have written to him to know what he has done with the
650 pounds &c. and for his accounts so long ago as five months.
Have no doubt, as he is a very honest man, that he will give, in

due time, a true account thereof. Meantime, as for money for your
children's support, the gentlemen have none in hand; but if they
had, it would make no difference, they being determined not to
pay a farthing without an order from chancery.
I am, Madam
For Mess. Ramsay and Shrimpshire,
Your humble servant,
Anthony Lambskin

Madam,
Am much surprised at your not sending up, as promised, the
end of the third volume of the new novel purchased by me. The
trade expects it at the time I notified to them that it would be
ready; and the printer informs me he shall stand still if not supplied immediately. Must insist on having a hondred pagges at
least by Satturday night; also the Ode to Liberty, mentioned by
you as a close to the same: but I shall change the tittle of that,
having promised the trade that there shall be no liberty at all in
the present work; without which asshurance they would not have
delt for the same.—Hopin to receive the manuscript (as you
have had money thereon,) at the time before-named, remain,
Madam, your humble servant,
Josephth Clapper
194, Holbourn,
Feb. 22, 17—

Such, my dear *****, are the delights that her existence
now affords to Mrs. Denzil, mingled and varied with others, of
which she will forbear to give a description, because you are not
ignorant of some, and others would only give you pain.
But to cease speaking in the second [*sic.* She must mean
third.] person—Do not *you*, my friend, add *your* censure to that
of the unfeeling triflers I have before described, and to many
others whom I *could* describe. Do not add your censure if I find

it always impossible to submit, without murmuring, to so dreary a fate; and let others, if they can a moment divest themselves of selfish prejudice, ask their own hearts whether *they* could acquit themselves better in circumstances like mine than I have done.

All, however, I could have borne, because I *must*—because I endured it for my children, and perhaps because I felt a degree of self-approbation in stemming a tide of adversity under which the generality of women would have sunk.—All this I could have endured with less disposition to murmur, did I not see, as I proceed in this rugged way, that those who now and then threw a flower before me, drop off as I go along—some from the mere weakness and caprice of human nature; others because I will not consent to consider it as proper to give up my understanding to their disposal; and some, alas! by death. You know how tenderly I was attached to one friend, thus torn from me . . . who supplied to me the many relations and connections that calamity has robbed me of—some by distance, and some by that estrangement which policy imposes on the sage and the prudent.

Notes

Desmond, PREFACE
Smith applies a slightly garbled quotation from William Shakespeare's *Hamlet* (III, i, 71–73) to her own experience of litigation over her children's inheritance. The other quotations are from Proverbs 13:12 and Shakespeare's *As You Like It,* II, ii, 12–14.

Desmond, FANNY WAVERLY'S LETTER
Serena was the heroine of William Hayley's *The Triumphs of Temper* (1781), a very popular book for ladies. The "mawkish reading" allowed to Fanny appears to be insipid love elegies in the manner of Sir Benjamin Backbite (Richard Brinsley Sheridan's *The School for Scandal* [1777], I, i) and, I suspect, Fanny Burney's *Evelina,* an epistolary novel in which Evelina, whose mother's maiden name was Evelyn, writes to her priggish guardian, Mr. Villars.

Desmond, DESMOND'S LETTER

James Boswell was relatively conservative.

Feeling against Negro slavery, and especially against the Slave Trade, had been building in England for some years, although the Slave Trade was not abolished until 1807. Years later, one of Charlotte Smith's sons, Lionel, distinguished himself by efforts on behalf of the slaves when he served as a governor in the West Indies.

James Burnett, Lord Monboddo, an eighteenth-century pioneer in anthropology, had drawn ridicule upon himself by arguing that man developed from the lower animals.

The Banished Man

"ci-devant"—former. The word was commonly applied to nobles who had lost their titles as a result of the French Revolution.

"les gens comme il faut"—well-bred people

"bookseller"—publisher

Samuel Richardson's Sir Charles Grandison was a model of masculine virtue; his Lovelace, the hero of *Clarissa,* a witty and attractive rake.

"dun"—debt collector

"pipe"—large cask, holding 126 gallons

"overseer"—parish officer in charge of administering poor relief

Bibliographical Note

Charlotte Smith published voluminously, chiefly multi-volume novels: *Emmeline, the Orphan of the Castle* (1788), *Ethelinde, or the Recluse of the Lake* (1789), *Celestina* (1791), *Desmond* (1792), *The Old Manor House* (1793), *The Wanderings of Warwick* (1794), *The Banished Man* (1794), *Montalbert* (1795), *Marchmont* (1796), *The Young Philosopher* (1798). In addition, she produced four volumes of poetry—*Elegiac Sonnets, and Other Essays* (1784), *The Emigrants* (1793), Volume II of *Elegiac Sonnets* (1797), *Beachy Head: with other poems* (1807)—a collection of short stories, translations, and children's books.

The only biography is Florence May Anna Hillbish's *Charlotte Smith, Poet and Novelist* (Philadelphia: University of Pennsylvania, 1941). Two of her novels, *Emmeline* and *The Old Manor House,* have been issued in the Oxford English Novels series, with introductions by

Anne Henry Ehrenpreis. Alan Dugald McKillop described a large group of her letters in "Charlotte Smith's Letters," *Huntington Library Quarterly*, *XV* (May 1952), 237–55. Katharine Rogers discussed her novels in "Inhibitions on Eighteenth-Century Women Novelists: Elizabeth Inchbald and Charlotte Smith," *Eighteenth-Century Studies*, XI (Fall 1977), 63–78.

FRANCES BURNEY D'ARBLAY

Frances Burney (1752–1840) was a painfully shy girl who had practically no systematic education. But she was part of a close group of sisters and brothers, and she had an unusually rich home environment; for the most eminent Londoners of the day regularly visited her father, Dr. Charles Burney, a fashionable and charming musician and a member of Samuel Johnson's circle. Quietly she observed them all and vividly recorded their conversation in her diary. She wrote constantly and had destroyed one entire novel before publishing *Evelina, or The History of a Young Lady's Entrance into the World* (1778). At first only a few relatives knew of her authorship, for she dreaded to disgrace herself and her father by failing in public. But the book proved a brilliant success, and she became a celebrity in the society of Johnson and the Bluestockings.

Evelina brought fame, but not fortune; and her family, seeing that she was not likely to marry, pressed her to repeat its success. After writing "The Witlings," a clever comedy on Bluestocking society which her elders considered indiscreet and persuaded her to suppress, she set to work on *Cecilia*, which appeared in 1782. This added to her fame but still did not provide financial security. Then Queen Charlotte offered her a position at Court as Second Keeper of the Robes. Under strong pressure from her adored father, she accepted it. She endured five years of hideous boredom and restraint until her father finally approved her retirement.

At the age of forty she fell in love with Alexandre d'Arblay, a penniless refugee from the French Revolution. She married him, over her father's protests, in 1793; and they were blissfully happy. They had one son. *Camilla,* published by subscription in 1796, earned her £2000 and established the family comfortably in Camilla Cottage. Then they lived in France for some years, since d'Arblay had no way of obtaining money in England. Returning home, she published her last novel, *The Wanderer, or Female Difficulties* (1814).

Evelina is a delightfully original book, bringing a fresh girlish point of view to the English novel. *Cecilia,* while overlong and often pompous in style, presents a more full and mature picture of society. But *Camilla* and *The Wanderer* sink under conventional moralizing and ponderous style. Burney is at her best in her diaries, where she reported what she saw and heard without feeling the need to moralize or to dignify her style. All her long life she kept voluminous journals, generally in the form of letters to her favorite sister, Susan (until Susan's death in 1800). The first excerpt given here shows Burney's continuing embarrassment at appearing as a writer and describes her first meetings with Johnson. The second, written after *Cecilia* was published, gives a vivid account of a fashionable London party. The third dramatizes her first meeting with the royal family. The last shows her after four weary years at Court.

FROM *DIARY*

Fanny Burney had published *Evelina* anonymously in January, only her aunts, sisters, brother, and a cousin knowing. Gradually other members of the family, friends, and acquaintances were let into the secret. Her father learned it on his own in July. Samuel Crisp of Chesington, so intimate a friend that she called him Daddy Crisp, has not yet learned the authorship.

Chesington, June 18th

Here I am, and here I have been this age; though too weak to think of journalizing; however, as I never had so many curious anecdotes to record, I will not, at least this year, the first of my appearing in public—give up my favourite old hobby-horse.

I came hither the first week in May. My recovery, from that time to this, has been slow and sure; but as I could walk hardly three yards in a day at first, I found so much time to spare, that I could not resist treating myself with a little private sport with *Evelina*, a young lady whom I think I have some right to make free with. I had promised *Hetty* that *she* should read it to Mr Crisp, at her own particular request; but I wrote my excuses, and introduced it myself.

I told him it was a book which Hetty had taken to Brompton, to divert my cousin Richard during his confinement. He was so indifferent about it, that I thought he would not give himself the trouble to read it, and often embarrassed me by unlucky questions, such as, 'If it was reckoned clever?' and 'What I thought of it?' and 'Whether folks laughed at it?' I always evaded any direct or satisfactory answer; but he was so totally free from any idea of suspicion, that my perplexity escaped his notice.

At length, he desired me to begin reading to him. I dared not trust my voice with the little introductory ode, for as *that* is no romance, but the sincere effusion of my heart, I could as soon read aloud my own letters, written in my own name and charac-

ter: I therefore skipped it, and have so kept the book out of his
sight, that, to this day, he knows not it is there. Indeed, I have,
since, heartily repented that I read *any* of the book to him, for I
found it a much more awkward thing than I had expected: my
voice quite faltered when I began it, which, however, I passed off
for the effect of remaining weakness of lungs; and, in short, from
an invincible embarrassment, which I could not for a page
together repress, the book, by my reading, lost all manner of
spirit.

Nevertheless, though he has by no means treated it with the
praise so lavishly bestowed upon it from other quarters, I had the
satisfaction to observe that he was even greedily eager to go on
with it; so that I flatter myself the *story* caught his attention:
and, indeed, allowing for my *mauling* reading, he gave it quite as
much credit as I had any reason to expect. But, now that I was
sensible of my error in being my own mistress of the ceremonies,
I determined to leave to Hetty the third volume, and therefore
pretended I had not brought it. He was in a delightful ill-hu-
mour about it, and I enjoyed his impatience far more than I
should have done his forbearance. Hetty, therefore, when she
comes, has undertaken to bring it.

Well, I cannot but rejoice that I published the book, little as
I ever imagined how it would fare; for hitherto it has occasioned
me no small diversion, and *nothing* of the disagreeable sort. But I
often think a change *will* happen, for I am by no means so sanguine as to suppose such success will be uninterrupted. Indeed, in
the midst of the greatest satisfaction that I feel, an inward *something* which I cannot account for, prepares me to expect a
reverse; for the more the book is drawn into notice, the more
exposed it becomes to criticism and remark.

July 25. Mrs Cholmondeley has been reading and praising
Evelina, and my father is quite delighted at her approbation, and
told Susan that I could not have had a greater compliment than
making two such women my friends as Mrs Thrale and Mrs Cholmondeley, for they were severe and knowing, and afraid of praising *à tort et à travers*, as their opinions are liable to be quoted.

Mrs Thrale said she had only to complain it was too short.

She recommended it to my mother to read!—how droll!—and she told her she would be much entertained with it, for there was a great deal of human life in it, and of the manners of the present times, and added that it was written 'by somebody who knows the top and the bottom, the highest and the lowest of mankind.' She has even lent her set to my mother, who brought it home with her!

August 3. I now come to last Saturday evening, when my beloved father came to Chesington, in full health, charming spirits, and all kindness, openness, and entertainment.

In his way hither he had stopped at Streatham, and he settled with Mrs Thrale that he would call on her again in his way to town, and carry me with him! and Mrs Thrale said: 'We all long to know her.'

I have been in a kind of twitter ever since, for there seems something very formidable in the idea of appearing as an authoress! I ever dreaded it, as it is a title which must raise more expectations than I have any chance of answering. Yet I am highly flattered by her invitation, and highly delighted in the prospect of being introduced to the Streatham society.

My dear father communicated this intelligence, and a great deal more, with a pleasure that almost surpassed that with which I heard it, and he seems quite eager for me to make another attempt. He desired to take upon himself the communication to my Daddy Crisp, and as it is now in so many hands that it is possible accident might discover it to him, I readily consented.

Sunday evening, as I was going into my father's room, I heard him say: 'The variety of characters—the variety of scenes —and the language—why she has had very little education but what she has given herself—less than any of the others!' and Mr Crisp exclaimed: 'Wonderful!—it's wonderful!'

I now found what was going forward, and therefore deemed it most fitting to decamp.

About an hour after, as I was passing through the hall, I met my daddy [Crisp]. His face was all animation and archness; he doubled his fist at me, and would have stopped me, but I ran past him into the parlour.

Before supper, however, I again met him, and he would not
suffer me to escape; he caught both my hands, and looked as if he
would have looked me through, and then exclaimed: 'Why, you
little hussy—you young devil!—an't you ashamed to look me in
the face, you *Evelina*, you! Why, what a dance have you led me
about it! Young friend, indeed! Oh, you little hussy, what tricks
have you served me!'

London, August. I have now to write an account of the most
consequential day I have spent since my birth; namely, my Streatham visit.

Our journey to Streatham was the least pleasant part of the
day, for the roads were dreadfully dusty, and I was really in the
fidgets from thinking what my reception might be, and from fear-
ing they would expect a less awkward and backward kind of
person that I was sure they would find.

Mr Thrale's house is white, and very pleasantly situated, in a
fine paddock. Mrs Thrale was strolling about, and came to us as
we got out of the chaise.

She then received me, taking both my hands, and with mixed
politeness and cordiality welcoming me to Streatham. She led me
into the house, and addressed herself almost wholly for a few
minutes to my father, as if to give me an assurance she did not
mean to regard me as a show, or to distress or frighten me by
drawing me out. Afterwards she took me upstairs, and showed me
the house, and said she had very much wished to see me at Streatham, and should always think herself much obliged to Dr Burney
for his goodness in bringing me, which she looked upon as a very
great favour.

But though we were some time together, and though she was
so very civil, she did not *hint* at my book, and I love her much
more than ever for her delicacy in avoiding a subject which she
could not but see would have greatly embarrassed me.

When we returned to the music room, we found Miss Thrale
was with my father. Miss Thrale is a very fine girl, about fourteen years of age, but cold and reserved, though full of knowledge
and intelligence.

Soon after, Mrs Thrale took me to the library; she talked a little while upon common topics, and then, at last, she mentioned *Evelina*.

'Yesterday at supper,' said she, 'we talked it all over, and discussed all your characters; but Dr Johnson's favourite is Mr Smith. He declares the fine gentleman *manqué* was never better drawn, and he acted him all the evening, saying "he was all for the ladies"! He repeated whole scenes by heart. I declare I was astonished at him. Oh, you can't imagine how much he is pleased with the book; he "could not get rid of the rogue," he told me. But was it not droll,' said she, 'that I should recommend to Dr Burney? and tease him so innocently to read it?'

I now prevailed upon Mrs Thrale to let me amuse myself, and she went to dress. I then prowled about to choose some book, and I saw, upon the reading-table, *Evelina*—I had just fixed upon a new translation of Cicero's *Laelius,* when the library door was opened, and Mr Seward entered. I instantly put away my book, because I dreaded being thought studious and affected. He offered his service to find anything for me, and then, in the same breath, ran on to speak of the book with which I had myself 'favoured the world'!

The exact words he began with I cannot recollect, for I was actually confounded by the attack; and his abrupt manner of letting me know he was *au fait* equally astonished and provoked me. How different from the delicacy of Mr and Mrs Thrale!

When we were summoned to dinner, Mrs Thrale made my father and me sit on each side of her. I said that I hoped I did not take Dr Johnson's place—for he had not yet appeared.

'No,' answered Mrs Thrale, 'he will sit by you, which I am sure will give him great pleasure.'

Soon after we were seated, this great man entered. I have so true a veneration for him, that the very sight of him inspires me with delight and reverence, notwithstanding the cruel infirmities to which he is subject; for he has almost perpetual convulsive movements, either of his hands, lips, feet, or knees, and sometimes all together.

Mrs Thrale introduced me to him, and he took his place. We

had a noble dinner, and a most elegant dessert. Dr Johnson, in the middle of dinner, asked Mrs Thrale what was in some little pies that were near him.

'Mutton,' answered she, 'so I don't ask you to eat any, because I know you despise it.'

'No, madam, no,' cried he; 'I despise nothing that is good of its sort; but I am too proud now to eat of it. Sitting by Miss Burney makes me very proud to-day!'

'Miss Burney,' said Mrs Thrale, laughing, 'you must take great care of your heart if Dr Johnson attacks it; for I assure you he is not often successless.'

'What's that you say, madam?' cried he; 'are you making mischief between the young lady and me already?'

A little while after he drank Miss Thrale's health and mine, and then added:

''Tis a terrible thing that we cannot wish young ladies well without wishing them to become old women!'

'But some people,' said Mr Seward, 'are old and young at the same time, for they wear so well that they never look old.'

'No, sir, no', cried the doctor, laughing; 'that never yet was; you might as well say they are at the same time tall and short. I remember an epitaph to that purpose, which is in——'

(I have quite forgot what—and also the name it was made upon, but the rest I recollect exactly:)

——— lies buried here;
So early wise, so lasting fair,
That none, unless her years you told,
Thought her a child, or thought her old.

Mrs Thrale then repeated some lines in French, and Dr Johnson some more in Latin. An epilogue of Mr Garrick's to *Bonduca* was then mentioned, and Dr Johnson said it was a miserable performance, and everybody agreed it was the worst he had ever made.

'And yet,' said Mr Seward, 'it has been very much admired; but it is in praise of English valour, and so I suppose the subject made it popular.'

'I don't know, sir,' said Dr Johnson, 'anything about the sub-

ject, for I could not read on till I came to it; I got through half a
dozen lines, but I could observe no other subject than eternal
dullness. I don't know what is the matter with David; I am afraid
he is grown superannuated, for his prologues and epilogues used
to be incomparable.'

'Nothing is so fatiguing,' said Mrs Thrale, 'as the life of a
wit; he and Wilkes are the two oldest men of their ages I know,
for they have both worn themselves out by being eternally on the
rack to give entertainment to others.'

'David, madam,' said the doctor, 'looks much older than he
is; for his face has had double the business of any other man's; it
is never at rest; when he speaks one minute, he has quite a different countenance to what he assumes the next; I don't believe he
ever kept the same look for half an hour together in the whole
course of his life; and such an eternal, restless, fatiguing play of
the muscles must certainly wear out a man's face before its real
time.'

'Oh, yes,' cried Mrs Thrale; 'we must certainly make some
allowance for such wear and tear of a man's face.'

We left Streatham at about eight o'clock, and Mr Seward,
who handed me into the chaise, added his interest to the rest,
that my father would not fail to bring me again next week to stay
with them for some time. In short, I was loaded with civilities
from them all. And my ride home was equally happy with the
rest of the day, for my kind and most beloved father was so
happy in *my* happiness, and congratulated me so sweetly, that he
could, like myself, think on no other subject.

Yet my honours stopped not here; for Hetty, who, with her
sposo, was here to receive us, told me she had lately met Mrs Reynolds, sister of Sir Joshua; and that she talked very much and
very highly of a new novel called *Evelina*; though without a
shadow of suspicion as to the scribbler; and not contented with
her own praise, she said that Sir Joshua, who began it one day
when he was too much engaged to go on with it, was so much
caught, that he could think of nothing else, and was quite absent
all the day, not knowing a word that was said to him: and, when
he took it up again, found himself so much interested in it, that
he sat up all night to finish it!

Sir Joshua, it seems, vows he would give fifty pounds to know the author! I have also heard, by the means of Charles, that other persons have declared they *will* find him out!

This intelligence determined me upon going myself to Mr Lowndes, and discovering what sort of answers he made to such curious inquirers as I found were likely to address him. But as I did not dare trust myself to speak, for I felt that I should not be able to act my part well, I asked my mother to accompany me.

We introduced ourselves by buying the book, for which I had a commission from Mrs G____. Fortunately Mr Lowndes himself was in the shop; as we found by his air of consequence and authority, as well as his age; for I never saw him before.

The moment he had given my mother the book, she asked if he could tell her who wrote it.

'No,' he answered; 'I don't know myself.'

'Pho, pho,' said she; 'you mayn't choose to tell, but you must know.'

'I don't, indeed, ma'am,' answered he; 'I have no honour in keeping the secret, for I have never been trusted. All I know of the matter is, that it is a gentleman of the other end of the town.'

My mother made a thousand other enquiries, to which his answers were to the following effect: that for a great while, he did not know if it was a man or a woman; but now, he knew that much, and that he was a master of his subject, and well versed in the manners of the times.

'For some time,' continued he, 'I thought it had been Horace Walpole's; for he once published a book in this snug manner; but I don't think it is now. I have often people come to inquire of me who it is; but I suppose he will come out soon, and then, when the rest of the world knows it, I shall. Servants often come for it from the other end of the town, and I have asked them divers questions myself, to see if I could get at the author; but I never got any satisfaction.'

Just before we came away, upon my mother's still further pressing him, he said, with a most important face:

'Why, to tell you the truth, madam, I have been informed that it is a piece of real secret history; and, in that case, it will never be known.'

This was too much for me; I grinned irresistibly, and was obliged to look out at the shop door till we came away.

Streatham, Sunday, Aug. 23. I know not how to express the fullness of my contentment at this sweet place. All my best expectations are exceeded, and you know they were not very moderate. If, when my dear father comes, Susan and Mr Crisp were to come too, I believe it would require at least a day's pondering to enable me to form another wish.

Our journey was charming. The kind Mrs Thrale would give courage to the most timid. She did not ask me questions, or catechize me upon what I knew, or use any means to draw me out, but made it her business to draw herself out—that is, to start subjects, to support them herself, and to take all the weight of the conversation, as if it behoved her to find me entertainment. But I am so much in love with her, that I shall be obliged to run away from the subject, or shall write of nothing else.

When we arrived here, Mrs Thrale showed me my room, which is an exceeding pleasant one, and then conducted me to the library, there to divert myself while she dressed.

Miss Thrale soon joined me: and I begin to like her. Mr Thrale was neither well nor in spirits all day. Indeed, he seems not to be a happy man, though he has every means of happiness in his power. But I think I have rarely seen a very rich man with a light heart and light spirits.

Dr Johnson was in the utmost good humour.

Saturday Morning. Dr Johnson was again all himself; and so civil to me!—even admiring how I dressed myself! Indeed, it is well I have so much of his favour; for it seems he always speaks his mind concerning the dress of ladies, and all ladies who are here obey his injunctions implicitly, and alter whatever he disapproves. This is a part of his character that much surprises me; but notwithstanding he is sometimes so absent, and always so near-sighted, he scrutinizes into every part of almost everybody's appearance. They tell me of a Miss Brown, who often visits here, and who has a slovenly way of dressing. 'And when she comes down in a morning,' says Mrs Thrale, 'her hair will be all loose, and her cap half off; and then Dr Johnson, who sees something is wrong, and does not know where the fault is, concludes it is in the cap, and says, "My dear, what do you wear such a vile cap for?" "I'll change it, sir," cries the poor girl, "if you don't like it." "Aye, do," he says; and away runs poor Miss Brown; but when she gets on another, it's the same thing, for the cap has nothing to do with the fault. And then she wonders that Dr Johnson should not like the cap, for she thinks it very pretty. And so on with her gown, which he also makes her change; but if the poor girl were to change through all her wardrobe, unless she could put her things on better, he would still find fault.'

And now let me try to recollect an account he gave us of certain celebrated ladies of his acquaintance: an account which, had you heard from himself, would have made you die with laughing, his manner is so peculiar, and enforces his humour so originally.

It was begun by Mrs Thrale's apologizing to him for troubling him with some question she thought trifling—Oh, I remember! We had been talking of colours, and of the fantastic names given to them, and why the palest lilac should be called *soupir étouffé*; and when Dr Johnson came in she applied to him.

'Why, madam,' said he, with wonderful readiness, 'it is called a stifled sigh because it is checked in its progress, and only half a colour.'

I could not help expressing my amazement at his universal readiness upon all subjects, and Mrs Thrale said to him:

'Sir, Miss Burney wonders at your patience with such stuff; but I tell her you are used to me, for I believe I torment you with more foolish questions than anybody else dares do.'

'No, madam,' said he, 'you don't torment me—you tease me, indeed, sometimes.'

'Aye, so I do, Dr Johnson, and I wonder you bear with my nonsense.'

'No, madam, you never talk nonsense; you have as much sense, and more wit, than any woman I know!'

'Oh,' cried Mrs Thrale, blushing, 'it is my turn . . . this morning, Miss Burney!'

'And yet," continued the doctor, with the most comical look, 'I have known all the wits, from Mrs Montagu down to Bet Flint!'

'Bet Flint!' cried Mrs Thrale; 'pray who is she?'

'Oh, a fine character, madam! She was habitually a slut and a drunkard, and occasionally a thief and a harlot.'

'And, for heaven's sake, how came you to know her?'

'Why, madam, she figured in the literary world, too! Bet Flint wrote her own life, and called herself Cassandra, and it was in verse; it began:

When Nature first ordain'd my birth,
A diminutive I was born on earth:
And then I came from a dark abode,
Into a gay and gaudy world.

So Bet brought me her verses to correct; but I gave her half a crown, and she liked it as well. Bet had a fine spirit; she advertised for a husband, but she had no success, for she told me no man aspired to her! Then she hired very handsome lodgings and a footboy; and she got a harpsichord, but Bet could not play; however, she put herself in fine attitudes, and drummed.'

Then he gave an account of another of these geniuses, who called herself by some fine name, I have forgotten what.

'She had not quite the same stock of virtue,' continued he, 'nor the same stock of honesty as Bet Flint; but I suppose she envied her accomplishments, for she was so little moved by the power of harmony, that while Bet Flint thought she was drumming very divinely, the other jade had her indicted for a nuisance!'

'And pray what became of her, sir?'

'Why, madam, she stole a quilt from the man of the house, and he had her taken up; but Bet Flint had a spirit not to be subdued; so when she found herself obliged to go to jail, she ordered a sedan-chair, and bid her footboy walk before her. However, the boy proved refractory, for he was ashamed, though his mistress was not.'

'And did she ever get out of jail again, sir?'

'Yes, madam; when she came to her trial, the judge acquitted her. "So now," she said to me, "the quilt is my own and now I'll make a petticoat of it." Oh, I loved Bet Flint!'

Oh, how we all laughed! Then he gave an account of another lady, who called herself Laurinda, and who also wrote verses and stole furniture; but he had not the same affection for her, he said, though she too 'was a lady who had high notions of honour.'

Then followed the history of another, who called herself Hortensia, and who walked up and down the park repeating a book of Virgil.

'But,' said he, 'though I know her story, I never had the good fortune to see her.'

After this he gave an account of the famous Mrs Pinketh-man; 'And she,' he said, 'told me she owed all her misfortunes to her wit; for she was so unhappy as to marry a man who thought himself also a wit, though I believe she gave him not implicit credit for it, but it occasioned much contradiction and ill-will.'

'Bless me, sir!' cried Mrs Thrale, 'how can all these vaga-bonds contrive to get at *you*, of all people?'

'Oh, the dear creatures!' cried he, laughing heartily, 'I can't but be glad to see them!'

'Why I wonder, sir, you never went to see Mrs Rudd among the rest?'

'Why, madam, I believe I should,' said he, 'if it was not for the newspapers; but I am prevented many frolics that I should like very well since I am become such a theme for the papers.'

Now would you ever have imagined this! Bet Flint, it seems, once took Kitty Fisher to see him, but to his no little regret he was not at home. 'And Mrs Williams,' he added, 'did not love Bet Flint, but Bet Flint made herself very easy about that.'

How Mr Crisp would have enjoyed this account! He gave it all with so droll a solemnity, and it was all so unexpected, that Mrs Thrale and I were both almost equally diverted.

December 8, 1782

Fanny Burney, supported by Mrs. and Miss Thrale, attends a fashionable party at the home of Mary Monckton, a noted

Bluestocking hostess. Her second novel, *Cecilia*, had come out in June. After commenting on the lack of ceremony with which they have been received, Burney describes the conversation:

Miss Monckton . . . kept her seat when [her guests] entered, and only turned round her head to nod it, and say: 'How do do?' after which they found what accommodation they could for themselves.

As soon, however, as she perceived Mrs and Miss Thrale, which was not till they had been some minutes in the room, she arose to welcome them, contrary to her general custom, and merely because it was their first visit. Our long trains making my entrance some time after theirs, gave me the advantage of being immediately seen by her, and she advanced to me with quickness, and very politely thanked me for coming, and said:

'I fear you think me very rude for taking the liberty of sending to you.'

'No, indeed, you did me much honour,' quoth I.

She then broke further into her general rules, by making way for me to a good place, and seating me herself, and then taking a chair next me, and beginning a little chat. I really felt myself much obliged to her for this seasonable attention, for I was presently separated from Mrs Thrale, and entirely surrounded by strangers, all dressed superbly, and all looking saucily; and as nobody's names were spoken, I had no chance to discover any acquaintances. Mr Metcalf, indeed, came and spoke to me the instant I came in, and I should have been very happy to have had him for my neighbour; but he was engaged in attending to Dr Johnson, who was standing near the fire, and environed with listeners.

Some new people now coming in, and placing themselves in a regular way, Miss Monckton exclaimed: 'My whole care is to prevent a circle'; and hastily rising, she pulled about the chairs, and planted the people in groups, with as dexterous a disorder as you would desire to see.

The company in general were dressed with more brilliancy than at any rout I ever was at, as most of them were going to the

Duchess of Cumberland's, and attired for that purpose. Just behind me sat Mrs Hampden, still very beautiful, but insufferably affected. Another lady, in full dress, and very pretty, came in soon after, and got herself a chair just before me; and then a conversation began between her and Mrs Hampden, of which I will give you a specimen.

'How disagreeable these sacques are! I am so incommoded with these nasty ruffles! I am going to Cumberland House—are you?'

'To be sure,' said Mrs Hampden; 'what else, do you think, would make me bear this weight of dress? I can't bear a sacque.'

'Why, I thought you said you should always wear them?'

'Oh, yes, but I have changed my mind since then—as many people do.'

'Well, I think it vastly disagreeable indeed,' said the other; 'you can't think how I'm encumbered with these ruffles!'

'Oh, I am quite oppressed with them,' said Mrs Hampden; 'I can hardly bear myself up.'

'And I dined in this way!' cried the other; 'only think—dining in a sacque!'

'Oh,' answered Mrs Hampden, 'it really puts me quite out of spirits.'

Well, have you enough?—and has my daddy raved enough?

Mrs and Miss Thrale had other engagements, and soon went away. Miss Monckton then took a chair again next to me, which she kept till we both started at the same voice, and she cried out: 'Oh, it's Mr Burke!' and she ran to him with as much joy as, if it had been our house, I should. Cause the second for liking her better.

I grew now in a violent fidget, both to have his notice, and for what his notice would be; but I sat very still, and he was seized upon by scores, and taken to another part of the room.

Then came in Sir Joshua Reynolds, and he soon drew a chair near mine, and from that time I was never without some friend at my elbow.

'Have you seen,' said he, 'Mrs Montagu lately?'

'No, not very lately.'

'But within these few months?'

'No, not since last year.'

'Oh, you must see her, then. You ought to see and to hear her—'twill be worth your while. Have you heard of the fine long letter she has written?'

'Yes, but I have not met with it.'

'I have.'

'And who is it to?'

'The old Duchess of Portland. She desired Mrs Montagu's opinion of *Cecilia*, and she has written it at full length. I was in a party at her Grace's, and heard of nothing but you. She is so delighted, and so sensibly, so rationally, that I only wish you could have heard her. And old Mrs Delany had been forced to begin it, though she had said she should never read any more; however, when we met, she was reading it already for the third time.'

Mr Burke very quietly came from Mrs Hampden, and sat down in the vacant place at my side. I could then wait no longer, for I found he was more near-sighted than myself; I, therefore, turned towards him and bowed; he seemed quite amazed, and really made me ashamed, however delighted, by the expressive civility and distinction with which he instantly rose to return my bow, and stood the whole time he was making his compliments upon seeing me, and calling himself the blindest of men for not finding me out sooner. And Mrs Burke, who was seated near me, said, loud enough for me to hear her:

'See, see! what a flirtation Mr Burke is beginning with Miss Burney! and before my face too!'

These ceremonies over, he sate down by me, and began a conversation which you, my dearest Susy, would be glad to hear, for my sake, word for word; but which I really could not listen to with sufficient ease, from shame at his warm eulogiums, to remember with any accuracy. The general substance, however, take as I recollect it.

After many most eloquent compliments upon the book, too delicate either to shock or sicken the nicest ear, he very emphatically congratulated me upon its most universal success; said: 'he was now too late to speak of it, since he could only echo the voice of the whole nation'; and added, with a laugh: 'I had hoped to have made some merit of my enthusiasm; but the moment I went about to hear what others say, I found myself merely one in a multitude.'

He then told me that, notwithstanding his admiration, he was the man who had dared to find some faults with so favourite and fashionable a work. I entreated him to tell me what they were and assured him nothing would make me so happy as to correct them under his direction. He then enumerated them: and I will tell you what they are, that you may not conclude I write nothing but the fairer part of my adventures, which I really always relate very honestly, though so fair they are at this time, that it hardly seems possible they should not be dressed up.

The masquerade he thought too long, and that something might be spared from Harrel's grand assembly; he did not like Morrice's part of the pantheon; and he wished the conclusion either more happy or more miserable; 'for in a work of imagination,' said he, 'there is no medium.'

I was not easy enough to answer him, or I have much, though perhaps not good for much, to say in defence of following life and nature as much in the conclusion as in the progress of a tale; and when is life and nature completely happy or miserable?

'But,' said he, when he had finished his comments, 'what excuse must I give for this presumption? I have none in the world to offer but the real, the high esteem I feel for you; and I must at the same time acknowledge it is all your own doing that I am able to find fault; for it is your general perfection in writing that has taught me to criticize where it is not quite uniform.'

Here's an orator, dear Susy!

Sir Joshua Reynolds now joined us.

'Are you telling her,' said he, 'of our conversation with the old wits? I am glad you hear of it from Mr Burke, Miss Burney, for he can tell it so much better than I can, and remember their very words.'

'Nothing else would they talk of for three whole hours,' said he, 'and we were there at the third reading of the bill.'

'I believe I was in good hands,' said I, 'if they talked of it to you?'

'Why, yes,' answered Sir Joshua, laughing, 'we joined in from time to time. Gibbon says he read the whole five volumes in a day.'

''Tis impossible,' cried Mr Burke, 'it cost me three days; and you know I never parted with it from the time I first opened it.'

Here are laurels, Susy! My dear daddy and Kitty, are you not doubly glad you so kindly hurried me upstairs to write when at Chesington?

December 16, 1785

Fanny Burney has met and come to love Mrs. Delany, who is a personal friend of the Royal Family and living in a house of theirs at Windsor, where they often drop in to see her. Burney is staying with Mrs. Delany. Mary Ann Port is Mrs. Delany's great-grand-niece, who lived with her; Bernard Dewes, her nephew.

After dinner, while Mrs Delany was left alone, as usual, to take a little rest—for sleep it but seldom proves—Mr B. Dewes, his little daughter, Miss Port, and myself, went into the drawing-room. And here, while, to pass the time, I was amusing the little girl with teaching her some Christmas games, in which her father and cousin joined, Mrs Delany came in. We were all in the middle of the room, and in some confusion—but she had but just come up to us to inquire what was going forwards, and I was disentangling myself from Miss Dewes, to be ready to fly off if any one knocked at the street door, when the door of the drawing-room was again opened, and a large man, in deep mourning, appeared at it, entering and shutting it himself without speaking.

A ghost could not more have scared me, when I discovered by its glitter on the black, a star! The general disorder had prevented his being seen, except by myself, who was always on the watch, till Miss P——, turning round, exclaimed: 'The King!— Aunt, the King!'

O mercy! thought I, that I were but out of the room! Which way shall I escape? And how to pass him unnoticed? There is but

the single door at which he entered, in the room! Every one
scampered out of the way: Miss P_____, to stand next the door;
Mr Bernard Dewes to a corner opposite it; his little girl clung to
me; and Mrs Delany advanced to meet his Majesty, who, after
quietly looking on till she saw him, approached, and inquired
how she did.

He then spoke to Mr Bernard, whom he had already met two
or three times here.

I had now retreated to the wall, and purposed gliding softly,
though speedily, out of the room; but before I had taken a single
step, the King, in a loud whisper to Mrs Delany, said: 'Is that
Miss Burney?' and on her answering: 'Yes, sir,' he bowed, and
with a countenance of the most perfect good humour, came close
up to me.

A most profound reverence on my part arrested the progress
of my intended retreat.

'How long have you been come back, Miss Burney?'

'Two days, sir.'

Unluckily he did not hear me, and repeated his question;
and whether the second time he heard me or not, I don't know,
but he made a little civil inclination of his head, and went back
to Mrs Delany.

He insisted she should sit down, though he stood himself,
and began to give her an account of the Princess Elizabeth, who
once again was recovering, and trying, at present, James's Powders.
She had been blooded, he said, twelve times in the last fortnight,
and had lost seventy-five ounces of blood, besides undergoing blis-
tering and other discipline. He spoke of her illness with the
strongest emotion, and seemed quite filled with concern for her
danger and sufferings.

Mrs Delany next inquired for the younger children. They
had all, he said, the whooping-cough, and were soon to be
removed to Kew.

'Not,' added he, 'for any other reason than change of air for
themselves; though I am pretty certain I have never had the distemper myself, and the Queen thinks she has not had it either—
we shall take our chance. When the two eldest had it, I sent them
away, and would not see them till it was over; but now there are

so many of them that there would be no end to separations, so I let it take its course.'

Mrs Delany expressed a good deal of concern at his running this risk, but he laughed at it, and said he was much more afraid of catching the rheumatism, which has been threatening one of his shoulders lately. However, he added, he should hunt the next morning, in defiance of it.

A good deal of talk then followed about his own health, and the extreme temperance by which he preserved it. The fault of his constitution, he said, was a tendency to excessive fat, which he kept, however, in order by the most vigorous exercise, and the strictest attention to a simple diet.

When Mrs Delany was beginning to praise his forbearance he stopped her.

'No, no,' he cried, ' 'tis no virtue; I only prefer eating plain and little, to growing diseased and infirm.'

When the discourse upon health and strength was over, the King went up to the table, and looked at a book of prints, from Claude Lorraine, which had been brought down for Miss Dewes; but Mrs Delany, by mistake, told him they were for me. He turned over a leaf or two, and then said:

'Pray, does Miss Burney draw, too?'

The *too* was pronounced very civilly.

'I believe not, sir,' answered Mrs Delany; 'at least, she does not tell.'

'Oh!' cried he, laughing, 'that's nothing! She is not apt to tell; she never does tell, you know! Her father told me that himself. He told me the whole history of her *Evelina*. And I shall never forget his face when he spoke of his feelings at first taking up the book!—he looked quite frightened, just as if he was doing it that moment! I never can forget his face while I live!'

Then coming up close to me, he said:

'But what?—what?—how was it?'

'Sir,' cried I, not well understanding him.

'How came you—how happened it?—what?—what?'

'I—I only wrote, sir, for my own amusement—only in some odd, idle hours.'

'But your publishing—your printing—how was that?'

'That was only, sir—only because _____'

I hesitated most abominably, not knowing how to tell him a long story, and growing terribly confused at these questions—besides, to say the truth, his own 'what? what?' so reminded me of those vile *Probationary Odes*, that, in the midst of all my flutter, I was really hardly able to keep my countenance.

The *What?* was then repeated with so earnest a look, that, forced to say something, I stammeringly answered:

'I thought—sir—it would look very well in print!'

I do really flatter myself this is the silliest speech I ever made! I am quite provoked with myself for it; but a fear of laughing made me eager to utter anything, and by no means conscious, till I had spoken, of what I was saying.

He laughed very heartily himself—well he might—and walked away to enjoy it, crying out:

'Very fair indeed! That's being very fair and honest!'

Then, returning to me again, he said:

'But your father—how came you not to show him what you wrote?'

'I was too much ashamed of it, sir, seriously.'

Literal truth that, I am sure.

'And how did he find it out?'

'I don't know myself, sir. He never would tell me.'

Literal truth again, my dear father, as you can testify.

'But how did you get it printed?'

'I sent it, sir, to a bookseller my father never employed, and that I never had seen myself, Mr. Lowndes, in full hope by that means he never would hear of it.'

'But how could you manage that?'

'By means of a brother, sir.'

'Oh!—you confided in a brother, then?'

'Yes, sir—that is, for publication.'

'What entertainment you must have had from hearing people's conjectures before you were known! Do you remember any of them?'

'Yes, sir, many.'

'And what?'

'I heard that Mr Baretti laid a wager it was written by a man; for no woman, he said, could have kept her own counsel.'

This diverted him extremely.

'But how was it,' he continued, 'you thought most likely for your father to discover you?'

'Sometimes, sir, I have supposed I must have dropped some of the manuscript: sometimes, that one of my sisters betrayed me.'

'Oh! your sister?—what, not your brother?'

'No sir; he could not, for ———'

I was going on, but he laughed so much I could not be heard, exclaiming:

'Vastly well! I see you are of Mr Baretti's mind, and think your brother could keep your secret, and not your sister.'

'Well, but,' cried he presently, 'how was it first known to you you were betrayed?'

'By a letter, sir, from another sister. I was very ill, and in the country; and she wrote me word that my father had taken up a review, in which the book was mentioned, and had put his finger upon its name, and said: "Contrive to get that book for me." '

'And when he got it,' cried the King, 'he told me he was afraid of looking at it! And never can I forget his face when he mentioned his first opening it. But you have not kept your pen unemployed all this time?'

'Indeed I have, sir,'

'But why?'

'I—I believe I have exhausted myself, sir.'

He laughed aloud at this, and went and told it to Mrs Delany, civilly treating a plain fact as a mere *bon mot*.

While this was talking over, a violent thunder was made at the door. I was almost certain it was the Queen. Once more I would have given anything to escape; but in vain. I had been informed that nobody ever quitted the royal presence, after having been conversed with, till motioned to withdraw.

Miss P———, according to established etiquette on these occasions, opened the door which she stood next, by putting her hand behind her, and slid out backwards into the hall, to light the Queen in. The door soon opened again, and her Majesty entered.

Immediately seeing the King, she made him a low curtsy, and cried:

'Oh, your Majesty is here!'

'Yes,' he cried, 'I ran here without speaking to anybody.'

The Queen had been at the lower Lodge, to see the Princess Elizabeth, as the King had before told us.

She then hastened up to Mrs Delany, with both her hands held out, saying:

'My dear Mrs Delany, how are you?'

Instantly after, I felt her eye on my face. I believe, too, she curtsied to me; but though I saw the bend, I was too near-sighted to be sure it was intended for me. I was hardly ever in a situation more embarrassing; I dared not return what I was not certain I had received, yet considered myself as appearing quite a monster, to stand stiffnecked, if really meant.

Almost at the same moment, she spoke to Mr Bernard Dewes, and then nodded to my little clinging girl.

I was now really ready to sink, with horrid uncertainty of what I was doing, or what I should do—when his Majesty, who I fancy saw my distress, most good-humouredly said to the Queen something, but I was too much flurried to remember what, except these words: 'I have been telling Miss Burney _____'

Relieved from so painful a dilemma, I immediately dropped a curtsy. She had made one to me in the same moment, and, with a very smiling countenance, came up to me, but she could not speak, for the King went on talking, eagerly, and very gaily repeating to her every word I had said during our conversation upon *Evelina*, its publication, etc., etc.

Then he told her of Baretti's wager, saying: 'But she heard of a great many conjectures about the author, before it was known, and of Baretti, an admirable thing! he laid a bet it must be a man, as no woman, he said, could have kept her own counsel!'

The Queen, laughing a little, exclaimed:

'Oh, that is quite too bad an affront to us! Don't you think so?' addressing herself to me, with great gentleness of voice and manner.

The King then went on, and when he had finished his narration the Queen took her seat.

She made Mrs Delany sit next her, and Miss P——— brought her some tea.

The King, meanwhile, came to me again, and said: 'Are you musical?'

'Not a performer, sir.'

Then, going from me to the Queen, he cried: 'She does not play.'

I did not hear what the Queen answered; she spoke in a low voice, and seemed much out of spirits.

They now talked together a little while, about the Princess Elizabeth, and the King mentioned having had a very promising account from her physician, Sir George Baker: and the Queen soon brightened up.

The King then returned to me, and said:

'Are you sure you never play? Never touch the keys at all?'

'Never to acknowledge it, sir.'

'Oh! that's it!' cried he; and flying to the Queen, cried: 'She does play—but not to acknowledge it!'

I was now in a most horrible panic once more; pushed so very home, I could answer no other than I did, for these categorical questions almost constrain categorical answers; and here, at Windsor, it seems an absolute point that whatever they ask must be told, and whatever they desire must be done. Think but, then, of my consternation, in expecting their commands to perform! My dear father, pity me!

The eager air with which he returned to me fully explained what was to follow. I hastily, therefore, spoke first, in order to stop him, crying: 'I never, sir, played to anybody but myself! Never!'

'No?' cried he, looking incredulous; 'what, not to ———'

'Not even to me, sir!' cried my kind Mrs Delany, who saw what was threatening me.

'No? Are you sure?' cried he, disappointed; 'but—but you'll ———'

'I have never, sir,' cried I, very earnestly, 'played in my life, but when I could hear nobody else—quite alone, and from a mere love of any musical sounds.'

He still, however, kept me in talk, and still upon music.

'To me,' said he, 'it appears quite as strange to meet with people who have no ear for music, and cannot distinguish one air from another, as to meet with people who are dumb. Lady Bell Finch once told me that she had heard there was some difference between a psalm, a minuet, and a country dance, but she declared they all sounded alike to her! There are people who have no eye for difference of colour. The Duke of Marlborough actually cannot tell scarlet from green!'

He then told me an anecdote of his mistaking one of those colours for another, which was very laughable, but I do not remember it clearly enough to write it. How unfortunate for true virtuosi that such an eye should possess objects worthy the most discerning—the treasures of Blenheim!

The King then, looking at his watch, said: 'It is eight o'clock, and if we don't go now, the children will be sent to the other house.'

'Yes, your Majesty,' cried the Queen, instantly rising.

Mrs Delany put on her Majesty's cloak, and she took a very kind leave of her. She then curtsied separately to us all, and the King handed her to the carriage.

It is the custom for everybody they speak to to attend them out, but they would not suffer Mrs Delany to move. Miss P——, Mr Dewes, and his little daughter, and myself, all accompanied them, and saw them in their coach, and received their last gracious nods.

When they were gone, Mrs Delany confessed she had heard the King's knock at the door before she came into the drawing-room, but would not avow it, that I might not run away. Well! being over was so good a thing, that I could not but be content.

October 1790

Fanny Burney has been at Court for four years, and everyone but her father and Queen Charlotte now realizes that she must quit the Queen's service to survive. William Windham has resolved to "set the Literary Club" upon Dr. Burney, and James Boswell, another member, will support his efforts. Boswell also tries to get information from Fanny for his *Life of Johnson*.

And now for a scene a little surprising.

The beautiful chapel of St George, repaired and finished by the best artists at an immense expense, which was now opened after a very long shutting up for its preparations, brought innumerable strangers to Windsor, and, among others, Mr Boswell.

This, I heard, in my way to the chapel, from Mr Turbulent, who overtook me, and mentioned having met Mr Boswell at the Bishop of Carlisle's the evening before. He proposed bringing him to call upon me; but this I declined, certain how little satisfaction would be given here by the entrance of a man so famous for compiling anecdotes. But yet I really wished to see him again, for old acquaintance' sake, and unavoidable amusement from his oddity and good humour, as well as respect for the object of his constant admiration, my revered Dr Johnson. I therefore told Mr Turbulent I should be extremely glad to speak with him after the service was over.

Accordingly, at the gate of the choir, Mr Turbulent brought him to me. We saluted with mutual glee: his comic-serious face and manner have lost nothing of their wonted singularity; nor yet have his mind and language, as you will soon confess.

'I am extremely glad to see you indeed,' he cried, 'but very sorry to see you here. My dear ma'am, why do you stay?—it won't do, ma'am! you must resign!—we can put up with it no longer. I told my good host the Bishop so last night; we are all grown quite outrageous!'

Whether I laughed the most, or stared the most, I am at a loss to say; but I hurried away from the cathedral, not to have such treasonable declarations overheard for we were surrounded by a multitude.

He accompanied me, however, not losing one moment in continuing his exhortations:

'If you do not quit, ma'am, very soon, some violent measures

I assure you, will be taken. We shall address Dr Burney in a body; I am ready to make the harangue myself. We shall fall upon him all at once.'

I stopped him to inquire about Sir Joshua; he said he saw him very often, and that his spirits were very good. I asked about Mr Burke's book.

'Oh,' cried he, 'it will come out next week: 'tis the first book in the world, except my own, and that's coming out also very soon; only I want your help.'

'My help?'

'Yes, madam; you must give me some of your choice little notes of the Doctor's; we have seen him long enough upon stilts; I want to show him in a new light. Grave Sam, and great Sam, and solemn Sam, and learned Sam—all these he has appeared over and over. Now I want to entwine a wreath of the graces across his brow; I want to show him as gay Sam, agreeable Sam, pleasant Sam; so you must help me with some of his beautiful billets to yourself.'

I evaded this by declaring I had not any stores at hand. He proposed a thousand curious expedients to get at them, but I was invincible.

Then I was hurrying on, lest I should be too late. He followed eagerly, and again exclaimed:

'But, ma'am, as I tell you, this won't do—you must resign off-hand! Why, I would farm you out myself for double, treble the money! I wish I had the regulation of such a farm—yet I am no farmer-general. But I should like to farm you, and so I will tell Dr Burney. I mean to address him; I have a speech ready for the first opportunity.'

He then told me his *Life of Dr Johnson* was nearly printed, and took a proof sheet out of his pocket to show me; with crowds passing and repassing, knowing me well, and staring well at him: for we were now at the iron rails of the Queen's Lodge.

I stopped; I could not ask him in: I saw he expected it, and was reduced to apologize, and tell him I must attend the Queen immediately.

He uttered again stronger and stronger exhortations for my retreat, accompanied by expressions which I was obliged to check in their bud. But finding he had no chance for entering, he stopped me again at the gate, and said he would read me a part of his work.

There was no refusing this; and he began, with a letter of Dr Johnson to himself. He read it in strong imitation of the Doctor's manner, very well, and not caricature. But Mrs Schwellenberg was at her window, a crowd was gathering to stand round the rails, and the King and Queen and Royal Family now approached from the Terrace. I made a rather quick apology, and, with a step as quick as my now weakened limbs have left in my power, I hurried to my apartment.

You may suppose I had inquiries enough, from all around, of 'Who was the gentleman I was talking to at the rails?' And an injunction rather frank not to admit him beyond those limits.

Notes

Diary, JUNE-AUGUST 1778
Hetty is Fanny's eldest sister; Susan, her dearest sister. Charles is the brother who negotiated the sale of *Evelina* to the publisher Thomas Lowndes, who remains ignorant of the author. Lowndes had published Horace Walpole's *The Castle of Otranto* anonymously (1764)— but there is no similarity between Walpole's work and Burney's. "My mother" is actually Fanny's stepmother.
"The little introductory ode" is an emotional effusion to her father. Mary Cholmondeley and Hester Thrale were female wits prominent in London society. Samuel Johnson, sixty-eight when Burney met him, spent much time during his later years at the Thrales' house at Streatham.
"à tort et à travers"—at random
Evelina features vulgar characters like the self-satisfied Mr. Smith.
David Garrick, the greatest actor of his time, frequently wrote prologues and epilogues for the plays he produced at Drury Lane. Jack Wilkes was noted both as a wit and a politician. Sir Joshua Reynolds, the leading portrait painter of his time, was, like Garrick and Fanny's father, a member of Johnson's Literary Club.

Elizabeth Montagu, a celebrated Bluestocking hostess, was called Queen of the Blues.

Margaret Caroline Rudd was tried for forgery and acquitted; the two brothers accused along with her were convicted and hanged.

Kitty Fisher was a famous prostitute.

Anna Williams was a blind lady whom Johnson supported in his house.

Diary, DECEMBER 8, 1782

"My whole care is to prevent a circle."—According to formal convention, the guests at a party like this sat in one large circle; more modern hostesses, like Miss Monckton, placed people in smaller groups in order to promote greater ease in conversation.

"sacque"—a loose-fitting dress with a train flowing from the shoulders.

Edmund Burke, a Whig politician and orator and a member of the Literary Club, was noted for his powerful intellect.

Mary Delany, known equally for her intelligence and her exquisite breeding, was a dear friend of the Duchess of Portland. Since they belonged to an earlier generation—Mrs. Delany was eighty-two—Reynolds refers to them as "the old wits."

Cecilia—The masquerade scene is overlong, though clever. Harrel is a prodigal with whom Cecilia becomes involved, and Morrice is a buffoon. The book ends happily, but only after a long sentimental scene in which the heroine, believing herself deserted, runs mad.

Edward Gibbon, the great historian, was another member of the Literary Club.

"Are you not doubly glad. . ."—Much of Cecilia was written at Chesington.

Diary, DECEMBER 16, 1785

Probationary Odes—King George III's mannerism of repeating "What" reminds Burney of the Probationary Odes for the Laureateship, satires issued by the Whigs on the death of William Whitehead, the Poet Laureate, in 1785, in which they pretended to compete for the vacant post. The specific allusion is to the lines:

> Methinks I hear,
> In accents clear,
> Great Brunswick's [George's] voice still vibrate on my ear:
> "What?—What?—What?"

Diary, OCTOBER 1790

Mr. Turbulent was Burney's private name for the Reverend Charles de Guiffardière, French reader to the Queen.

Burke's book was *Reflections on the Revolution in France,* which came
out in November.
Elizabeth Schwellenberg, Keeper of the Robes, an unreasonable and
tyrannical woman, was Burney's immediate superior.

Bibliographical Note

Frances Burney d'Arblay published novels—*Evelina* (1778), *Cecilia*
(1782), *Camilla* (1796), and *The Wanderer* (1814)—and *The Memoirs
of Dr. Burney* (1832). "The Witlings" and her other plays exist in manuscript in the Berg Collection at the New York Public Library.

Her *Diary and Letters,* edited by her niece Charlotte Barrett, were
published in seven volumes in 1842 to 1846. Her *Early Diary, 1768–78,*
edited by Annie Raine Ellis, was published in two volumes in 1889.
There have been several subsequent editions, some adding new material.
Joyce Hemlow is bringing out a new, complete edition of *The Journals
and Letters,* from 1791 on (Oxford: Clarendon, 1972–).

The authoritative biography is Joyce Hemlow's *The History of
Fanny Burney* (Oxford: Clarendon, 1958). For critical discussion of
the novels, see David Cecil, *Poets and Story-Tellers* (New York: Barnes
and Noble, n.d.), Bridget G. MacCarthy, *The Female Pen: The Later
Women Novelists 1744–1818* (Cork: University Press, 1947), Patricia M.
Spacks, *The Female Imagination* (New York: Alfred A. Knopf, 1975),
and Harrison R. Steeves, *Before Jane Austen* (New York: Holt, Rine-
hart, and Winston, 1965).

MARY WOLLSTONECRAFT GODWIN

Mary Wollstonecraft (1759–1797), growing up with an improvident, brutal father and a weak mother, knew at first hand the oppression of women in her society. After working as a companion, a schoolmistress, and a governess, she became a professional writer. She published a mildly feminist sentimental novel, *Mary: A Fiction* (1788), and wrote extensively for *The Analytical Review,* a magazine established by her publisher, Joseph Johnson. At Johnson's home she met radical thinkers such as Thomas Paine and William Godwin. Godwin, who was to establish himself as the leading radical theorist of his day with his *Enquiry Concerning Political Justice* (1793), was not favorably impressed at their first meeting, when he found her talkative and opinionated: "I heard her very frequently, when I wished to hear Paine." She published the first answer to Edmund Burke's *Reflections on the Revolution in France, A Vindication of the Rights of Men* (1790), and logically progressed to *A Vindication of the Rights of Woman* (1792).

She went to Paris to observe the French Revolution at first hand and to gather material for a history which would justify it. There she fell in love with Gilbert Imlay, an American entrepreneur, to whom she bore a daughter. They returned to London, and she went to Scandinavia on a business trip for Imlay, which led to her engaging travel book, *Letters Written During a Short Residence in Sweden, Norway, and Denmark.* Finding on her return that Imlay was living with another woman, she attempted suicide; but Joseph Johnson persuaded her to make a fresh start.

She saw Godwin again, and they fell in love. For seven months they lived as lovers, keenly enjoying each other's society though maintaining separate households; but when she became pregnant they overcame their theoretical objections to marriage for the sake of the coming child. Meanwhile she started a novel, *Maria, or The Wrongs of Woman*, which unfortunately remains only a promising fragment. For, eleven days after giving birth to her daughter Mary (the future wife of Percy Bysshe Shelley), she died of obstetrical complications.

A Vindication of the Rights of Woman shows the emphasis on independence, dislike of group privilege, and refusal uncritically to accept traditional views of right which were characteristic of contemporary radical thinkers. But few of them extended these principles as Wollstonecraft did, to women. Her dedication of her book to Charles Maurice de Talleyrand-Périgord reflects her keen disappointment that he, along with most other French Revolutionary leaders, ignored the rights of women in their plans for a new and reformed society. In Chapter II she trenchantly attacks the prevailing assumption of her time that women are morally different from men, with their own particular virtues and ends, distinct from the general human standard; she demonstrates that this separate standard serves to rationalize the subjection of women and must be swept away so they can become equal human beings.

A VINDICATION OF THE RIGHTS OF WOMAN

Dedication

TO M. TALLEYRAND-PERIGORD,
LATE BISHOP OF AUTUN.

Sir,—Having read with great pleasure a pamphlet which you have lately published, I dedicate this volume to you; to induce you to reconsider the subject, and maturely weigh what I have advanced respecting the rights of woman and national education: and I call with the firm tone of humanity; for my arguments, sir, are dictated by a disinterested spirit—I plead for my sex—not for myself. Independence I have long considered as the grand blessing of life, the basis of every virtue—and independence I will ever secure by contracting my wants, though I were to live on a barren heath.

It is then an affection for the whole human race that makes my pen dart rapidly along to support what I believe to be the cause of virtue; and the same motive leads me earnestly to wish to see woman placed in a station in which she would advance, instead of retarding, the progress of those glorious principles that give a substance to morality. My opinion, indeed, respecting the rights and duties of woman, seems to flow so naturally from these simple principles, that I think it scarcely possible, but that some of the enlarged minds who formed your admirable constitution will coincide with me.

In France there is undoubtedly a more general diffusion of knowledge than in any part of the European world, and I attribute it, in a great measure, to the social intercourse which has long subsisted between the sexes. It is true, I utter my sentiments with freedom, that in France the very essence of sensuality has been extracted to regale the voluptuary, and a kind of sentimental lust has prevailed, which, together with the system of duplicity that the whole tenor of their political and civil government taught, have given a sinister sort of sagacity to the French character, properly termed finesse; from which naturally flow a polish of manners that injures the substance, by hunting sincerity out of society. And, modesty, the fairest garb of virtue! has been more grossly insulted in France than even in England, till their women have treated as *prudish* that attention to decency which brutes instinctively observe.

Manners and morals are so nearly allied that they have often been confounded; but, though the former should only be the natural reflection of the latter, yet, when various causes have produced factitious and corrupt manners, which are very early caught, morality becomes an empty name. The personal reserve, and sacred respect for cleanliness and delicacy in domestic life, which French women almost despise, are the graceful pillars of modesty; but, far from despising them, if the pure flame of patriotism have reached their bosoms, they should labour to improve the morals of their fellow-citizens, by teaching men, not only to respect modesty in women, but to acquire it themselves, as the only way to merit their esteem.

Contending for the rights of woman, my main argument is built on this simple principle, that if she be not prepared by education to become the companion of man, she will stop the progress of knowledge and virtue; for truth must be common to all, or it will be inefficacious with respect to its influence on general practice. And how can woman be expected to co-operate unless she know why she ought to be virtuous? unless freedom strengthen her reason till she comprehend her duty, and see in what manner it is connected with her real good? If children are to be educated to understand the true principle of patriotism, their mother must be a patriot; and the love of mankind, from which an orderly train of virtues spring, can only be produced by considering the moral and civil interest of mankind; but the education and situation of woman, at present, shuts her out from such investigations.

In this work I have produced many arguments, which to me were conclusive, to prove that the prevailing notion respecting a sexual character was subversive of morality, and I have contended, that to render the human body and mind more perfect, chastity must more universally prevail, and that chastity will never be respected in the male world till the person of a woman is not, as it were, idolized, when little virtue or sense embellish it with the grand traces of mental beauty, or the interesting simplicity of affection.

Consider, sir, dispassionately, these observations—for a glimpse of this truth seemed to open before you when you observed, "that to see one half of the human race excluded by the other from all participation of government, was a political phenomenon that, according to abstract principles, it was impossible to explain." If so, on what does your constitution rest? If the abstract rights of man will bear discussion and explanation, those of woman, by a parity of reasoning, will not shrink from the same test: though a different opinion prevails in this country, built on the very arguments which you use to justify the oppression of woman—prescription.

Consider—I address you as a legislator—whether, when men contend for their freedom, and to be allowed to judge for themselves respecting their own happiness, it be not inconsistent and unjust to subjugate women, even though you firmly believe that you are acting in the manner best calculated to promote their happiness? Who made man the exclusive judge, if woman partake with him the gift of reason?

In this style, argue tyrants of every denomination, from the weak king to the weak father of a family; they are all eager to crush reason; yet always assert that they usurp its throne only to be useful. Do you not act a similar part, when you *force* all women, by denying them civil and political rights, to remain immured in their families groping in the dark? for surely, sir, you will not assert that a duty can be binding which is not founded on reason? If indeed this be their destination, arguments may be drawn from reason: and thus augustly supported, the more understanding women acquire, the more they will be attached to their duty—comprehending it—for unless they comprehend it, unless their morals be fixed on the same immutable principle as those of man, no authority can make them discharge it in a virtuous manner. They may be convenient slaves, but slavery will have its constant effect, degrading the master and the abject dependent.

But, if women are to be excluded without having a voice, from a participation of the natural rights of mankind, prove first, to ward off the charge of injustice and inconsistency, that they want reason—else this flaw in your NEW CONSTITUTION will ever show that man must, in some shape, act like a tyrant; and tyranny, in whatever part of society it rears its brazen front, will ever undermine morality.

I have repeatedly asserted, and produced what appeared to me irrefragable arguments drawn from matters of fact, to prove my assertion, that women cannot, by force, be confined to domestic concerns; for they will, however ignorant, intermeddle with more weighty affairs, neglecting private duties only to disturb, by cunning tricks, the orderly plans of reason which rise above their comprehension.

Besides, whilst they are only made to acquire personal accomplishments, men will seek for pleasure in variety, and faithless husbands will make faithless wives: such ignorant beings, indeed, will be very excusable when, not taught to respect public good, nor allowed any civil rights, they attempt to do themselves justice by retaliation.

The box of mischief thus opened in society, what is to preserve private virtue, the only security of public freedom and universal happiness?

Let there be then no coercion *established* in society, and the common law of gravity prevailing, the sexes will fall into their proper places. And, now that more equitable laws are forming your citizens, marriage may become more sacred: your young men may choose wives from motives of affection, and your maidens allow love to root out vanity.

The father of a family will not then weaken his constitution and debase his sentiments by visiting the harlot, nor forget, in obeying the call of appetite, the purpose for which it was implanted. And, the mother will not neglect her children to prac- tise the arts of coquetry, when sense and modesty secure her the friendship of her husband.

But, till men become attentive to the duty of a father, it is vain to expect women to spend that time in their nursery which they, "wise in their generation," choose to spend at their glass; for this exertion of cunning is only an instinct of nature to enable them to obtain indirectly a little of that power of which they are unjustly denied a share: for, if women are not permitted to enjoy legitimate rights, they will render both men and them- selves vicious, to obtain illicit privileges.

I wish, sir, to set some investigations of this kind afloat in France; and should they lead to a confirmation of my principles, when your constitution is revised the Rights of Women may be respected, if it be fully proved that reason calls for this respect, and loudly demands JUSTICE for one half of the human race.— I am, sir, yours respectfully,

                                                                    M.W.

Chapter II

THE PREVAILING OPINION
OF A SEXUAL CHARACTER DISCUSSED

To account for, and excuse the tyranny of man, many ingen- ious arguments have been brought forward to prove, that the two sexes, in the acquirement of virtue, ought to aim at attaining a very different character; or, to speak explicitly, women are not allowed to have sufficient strength of mind to acquire what really deserves the name of virtue. Yet it should seem, allowing them to have souls, that there is but one way appointed by Providence to lead *mankind* to either virtue or happiness.

If then women are not a swarm of ephemeron triflers, why should they be kept in ignorance under the specious name of innocence? Men complain, and with reason, of the follies and caprices of our sex, when they do not keenly satirize our head-strong passions and grovelling vices. Behold, I should answer, the natural effect of ignorance! The mind will ever be unstable that has only prejudices to rest on, and the current will run with destructive fury when there are no barriers to break its force. Women are told from their infancy, and taught by the example of their mothers, that a little knowledge of human weakness, justly termed cunning, softness of temper, *outward* obedience, and a scrupulous attention to a puerile kind of propriety, will obtain for them the protection of man; and should they be beautiful, everything else is needless, for, at least, twenty years of their lives.

Thus Milton describes our first frail mother; though when he tells us that women are formed for softness and sweet attractive grace, I cannot comprehend his meaning, unless, in the true Mahometan strain, he meant to deprive us of souls, and insinuate that we were beings only designed by sweet attractive grace, and docile blind obedience, to gratify the senses of man when he can no longer soar on the wing of contemplation.

How grossly do they insult us who thus advise us only to render ourselves gentle, domestic brutes! For instance, the winning softness so warmly, and frequently, recommended, that governs by obeying. What childish expressions, and how insignificant is the being—can it be an immortal one? who will condescend to govern by such sinister methods! "Certainly," says Lord Bacon, "man is of kin to the beasts by his body; and if he be not of kin to God by his spirit, he is a base and ignoble creature!" Men, indeed, appear to me to act in a very unphilosophical manner when they try to secure the good conduct of women by attempting to keep them always in a state of childhood. Rousseau was more consistent when he wished to stop the progress of reason in both sexes, for if men eat of the tree of knowledge, women will come in for a taste; but, from the imperfect cultivation which their understandings now receive, they only attain a knowledge of evil.

Children, I grant, should be innocent; but when the epithet is applied to men, or women, it is but a civil term for weakness. For if it be allowed that women were destined by Providence to acquire human virtues, and by the exercise of their understanding, that stability of character which is the firmest ground to rest our future hopes upon, they must be permitted to turn to the fountain of light, and not forced to shape their course by the twinkling of a mere satellite. Milton, I grant, was of a very different opinion; for he only bends to the indefeasible right of beauty, though it would be difficult to render two passages which I now mean to contrast, consistent. But into similar inconsistencies are great men often led by their senses.

> To whom thus Eve with *perfect beauty* adorn'd.
> My Author and Disposer, what thou bidst
> *Unargued* I obey; so God ordains;
> God is *thy law, thou mine:* to know no more
> Is Woman's *happiest* knowledge and her *praise.*

These are exactly the arguments that I have used to children; but I have added, your reason is now gaining strength, and, till it arrives at some degree of maturity, you must look up to me for advice—then you ought to *think,* and only rely on God.

Yet in the following lines Milton seems to coincide with me; when he makes Adam thus expostulate with his Maker.

> Hast thou not made me here thy substitute,
> And these inferior far beneath me set?
> Among *unequals* what society
> Can sort, what harmony or true delight?
> Which must be mutual, in proportion due
> Giv'n and receiv'd; but in *disparity*
> The one intense, the other still remiss
> Cannot well suit with either, but soon prove
> Tedious alike: of *fellowship* I speak

Such as I seek, fit to participate
All rational delight—

In treating, therefore, of the manners of women, let us, disregarding sensual arguments, trace what we should endeavour to make them in order to co-operate, if the expression be not too bold, with the supreme Being.

By individual education, I mean, for the sense of the word is not precisely defined, such an attention to a child as will slowly sharpen the senses, form the temper, regulate the passions as they begin to ferment, and set the understanding to work before the body arrives at maturity; so that the man may only have to proceed, not to begin, the important task of learning to think and reason.

To prevent any misconstruction, I must add, that I do not believe that a private education can work the wonders which some sanguine writers have attributed to it. Men and women must be educated, in a great degree, by the opinions and manners of the society they live in. In every age there has been a stream of popular opinion that has carried all before it, and given a family character, as it were, to the century. It may then fairly be inferred, that, till society be differently constituted, much cannot be expected from education. It is, however, sufficient for my present purpose to assert, that, whatever effect circumstances have on the abilities, every being may become virtuous by the exercise of its own reason; for if but one being was created with vicious inclinations, that is positively bad, what can save us from atheism? or if we worship a God, is not that God a devil?

Consequently, the most perfect education, in my opinion, is such an exercise of the understanding as is best calculated to strengthen the body and form the heart. Or, in other words, to enable the individual to attain such habits of virtue as will render it independent. In fact, it is a farce to call any being virtuous whose virtues do not result from the exercise of its own reason. This was Rousseau's opinion respecting men: I extend it to women, and confidently assert that they have been drawn out of their sphere by false refinement, and not by an endeavour to acquire masculine qualities. Still the regal homage which they receive is so intoxicating, that till the manners of the times are changed, and formed on more reasonable principles, it may be impossible to convince them that the illegitimate power, which they obtain, by degrading themselves, is a curse, and that they must return to nature and equality, if they wish to secure the placid satisfaction that unsophisticated affections impart. But for this epoch we must wait—wait, perhaps, till kings and nobles, enlightened by reason, and, preferring the real dignity of man to childish state, throw off their gaudy hereditary trappings: and if then women do not resign the arbitrary power of beauty—they will prove that they have *less* mind than man.

I may be accused of arrogance; still I must declare what I firmly believe, that all the writers who have written on the subject of female education and manners, from Rousseau to Dr. Gregory, have contributed to render women more artificial, weak characters, than they would otherwise have been; and consequently, more useless members of society. I might have expressed this conviction in a lower key; but I am afraid it would have been the whine of affectation, and not the faithful expression of my feelings, of the clear result which experience and reflection have led me to draw. When I come to that division of the subject, I shall advert to the passages that I more particularly disapprove of, in the works of the authors I have just alluded to; but it is first necessary to observe, that my objection extends to the whole purport of those books, which tend, in my opinion, to degrade one half of the human species, and render women pleasing at the expense of every solid virtue.

Though, to reason on Rousseau's ground, if man did attain a degree of perfection of mind when his body arrived at maturity, it might be proper, in order to make a man and his wife *one*, that she should rely entirely on his understanding; and the graceful ivy, clasping the oak that supported it, would form a whole in which strength and beauty would be equally conspicuous. But, alas! husbands, as well as their helpmates, are often only overgrown children; nay, thanks to early debauchery, scarcely men in their outward form—and if the blind lead the blind, one need not come from heaven to tell us the consequence.

Many are the causes that, in the present corrupt state of

society, contribute to enslave women by cramping their understandings and sharpening their senses. One, perhaps, that silently
does more mischief than all the rest, is their disregard of order.

To do everything in an orderly manner, is a most important
precept, which women, who, generally speaking, receive only a
disorderly kind of education, seldom attend to with that degree
of exactness that men, who from their infancy are broken into
method, observe. This negligent kind of guess-work, for what
other epithet can be used to point out the random exertions of a
sort of instinctive common sense, never brought to the test of
reason? prevents their generalizing matters of fact—so they do to-
day, what they did yesterday, merely because they did it yesterday.

This contempt of the understanding in early life has more
baneful consequences than is commonly supposed; for the little
knowledge which women of strong minds attain, is, from various
circumstances, of a more desultory kind than the knowledge of
men, and it is acquired more by sheer observations on real life,
than from comparing what has been individually observed with
the results of experience generalized by speculation. Led by their
dependent situation and domestic employments more into
society, what they learn is rather by snatches; and as learning is
with them, in general, only a secondary thing, they do not pursue
any one branch with that persevering ardour necessary to give
vigour to the faculties, and clearness to the judgment. In the present state of society, a little learning is required to support the
character of a gentleman; and boys are obliged to submit to a few
years of discipline. But in the education of women, the cultivation of the understanding is always subordinate to the acquirement of some corporeal accomplishment; even while enervated by
confinement and false notions of modesty, the body is prevented
from attaining that grace and beauty which relaxed half-formed
limbs never exhibit. Besides, in youth their faculties are not
brought forward by emulation; and having no serious scientific
study, if they have natural sagacity it is turned too soon on life
and manners. They dwell on effects, and modifications, without
tracing them back to causes; and complicated rules to adjust
behaviour are a weak substitute for simple principles.

As a proof that education gives this appearance of weakness to females, we may instance the example of military men, who are, like them, sent into the world before their minds have been stored with knowledge or fortified by principles. The consequences are similar; soldiers acquire a little superficial knowledge, snatched from the muddy current of conversation, and, from continually mixing with society, they gain, what is termed a knowledge of the world; and this acquaintance with manners and customs has frequently been confounded with a knowledge of the human heart. But can the crude fruit of casual observation, never brought to the test of judgment, formed by comparing speculation and experience, deserve such a distinction? Soldiers, as well as women, practice the minor virtues with punctilious politeness. Where is then the sexual difference, when the education has been the same? All the difference that I can discern, arises from the superior advantage of liberty, which enables the former to see more of life.

It is wandering from my present subject, perhaps, to make a political remark; but, as it was produced naturally by the train of my reflections, I shall not pass it silently over.

Standing armies can never consist of resolute robust men; they may be well disciplined machines, but they will seldom contain men under the influence of strong passions, or with very vigorous faculties. And as for any depth of understanding, I will venture to affirm, that it is as rarely to be found in the army as amongst women; and the cause, I maintain, is the same. It may be further observed, that officers are also particularly attentive to their persons, fond of dancing, crowded rooms, adventures, and ridicule. Like the *fair* sex, the business of their lives is gallantry. They were taught to please, and they only live to please. Yet they do not lose their rank in the distinction of sexes, for they are still reckoned superior to women, though in what their superiority consists, beyond what I have just mentioned, it is difficult to discover.

The great misfortune is this, that they both acquire manners before morals, and a knowledge of life before they have, from reflection, any acquaintance with the grand ideal outline of human nature. The consequence is natural; satisfied with common nature, they become a prey to prejudices, and taking all their opinions on credit, they blindly submit to authority. So that, if they have any sense, it is a kind of instinctive glance, that catches proportions, and decides with respect to manners; but fails when arguments are to be pursued below the surface, or opinions analyzed.

May not the same remark be applied to women? Nay, the argument may be carried still further, for they are both thrown out of a useful station by the unnatural distinctions established in civilized life. Riches and hereditary honours have made cyphers of women to give consequence to the numerical figure; and idleness has produced a mixture of gallantry and despotism into society, which leads the very men who are the slaves of their mistresses to tyrannize over their sisters, wives, and daughters. This is only keeping them in rank and file, it is true. Strengthen the female mind by enlarging it, and there will be an end to blind obedience; but, as blind obedience is ever sought for by power, tyrants and sensualists are in the right when they endeavour to keep women in the dark, because the former only want slaves, and the latter a plaything. The sensualist, indeed, has been the most dangerous of tyrants, and women have been duped by their lovers, as princes by their ministers, whilst dreaming that they reigned over them.

I now principally allude to Rousseau, for his character of Sophia is, undoubtedly, a captivating one, though it appears to me grossly unnatural; however it is not the superstructure, but the foundation of her character, the principles on which her education was built, that I mean to attack; nay, warmly as I admire the genius of that able writer, whose opinions I shall often have occasion to cite, indignation always takes place of admiration, and the rigid frown of insulted virtue effaces the smile of complacency, which his eloquent periods are wont to raise, when I read his voluptuous reveries. Is this the man, who, in his ardour for virtue, would banish all the soft arts of peace, and almost carry us back to Spartan discipline? Is this the man who delights to paint the useful struggles of passion, the triumphs of good dispositions, and the heroic flights which carry the glowing soul out of itself? —How are these mighty sentiments lowered when he describes the pretty foot and enticing airs of his little favourite! But, for the present, I waive the subject, and, instead of severely repre- hending the transient effusions of overweening sensibility, I shall only observe, that whoever has cast a benevolent eye on society, must often have been gratified by the sight of humble mutual love, not dignified by sentiment, or strengthened by a union in intellectual pursuits. The domestic trifles of the day have afforded matters for cheerful converse, and innocent caresses have softened toils which did not require great exercise of mind or stretch of thought: yet, has not the sight of this moderate felicity excited more tenderness than respect? An emotion similar to what we feel when children are playing, or animals sporting, whilst the contemplation of the noble struggles of suffering merit has raised admiration, and carried our thoughts to that world where sensation will give place to reason.

Women are, therefore, to be considered either as moral beings, or so weak that they must be entirely subjected to the superior faculties of men.

Let us examine this question. Rousseau declares that a woman should never, for a moment, feel herself independent, that she should be governed by fear to exercise her *natural* cun- ning, and made a coquettish slave in order to render her a more alluring object of desire, a *sweeter* companion to man, whenever he chooses to relax himself. He carries the arguments, which he pretends to draw from the indications of nature, still further, and insinuates that truth and fortitude, the corner stones of all human virtue, should be cultivated with certain restrictions, because, with respect to the female character, obedience is the grand lesson which ought to be impressed with unrelenting rigour.

What nonsense! when will a great man arise with sufficient strength of mind to puff away the fumes which pride and sensual- ity have thus spread over the subject! If women are by nature inferior to men, their virtues must be the same in quality, if not in degree, or virtue is a relative idea; consequently, their conduct should be founded on the same principles, and have the same aim.

Connected with man as daughters, wives, and mothers, their moral character may be estimated by their manner of fulfilling those simple duties; but the end, the grand end of their exertions should be to unfold their own faculties and acquire the dignity of conscious virtue. They may try to render their road pleasant; but ought never to forget, in common with man, that life yields not the felicity which can satisfy an immortal soul. I do not mean to insinuate that either sex should be so lost in abstract reflections or distant views, as to forget the affections and duties that lie before them, and are, in truth, the means appointed to produce the fruit of life; on the contrary, I would warmly recommend them, even while I assert, that they afford most satisfaction when they are considered in their true, sober light.

Probably the prevailing opinion, that woman was created for man, may have taken its rise from Moses's poetical story; yet, as very few, it is presumed, who have bestowed any serious thought on the subject, ever supposed that Eve was, literally speaking, one of Adam's ribs, the deduction must be allowed to fall to the ground; or, only be so far admitted as it proves that man, from the remotest antiquity, found it convenient to exert his strength to subjugate his companion, and his invention to show that she ought to have her neck bent under the yoke, because the whole creation was only created for his convenience or pleasure.

Let it not be concluded that I wish to invert the order of things; I have already granted, that, from the constitution of their bodies, men seem to be designed by Providence to attain a greater degree of virtue. I speak collectively of the whole sex; but I see not the shadow of a reason to conclude that their virtues should differ in respect to their nature. In fact, how can they, if virtue has only one eternal standard? I must therefore, if I reason consequentially, as strenuously maintain that they have the same simple direction, as that there is a God.

It follows then that cunning should not be opposed to wisdom, little cares to great exertions, or insipid softness, varnished over with the name of gentleness, to that fortitude which grand views alone can inspire.

I shall be told that woman would then lose many of her

peculiar graces, and the opinion of a well known poet might be quoted to refute my unqualified assertion. For Pope has said, in the name of the whole male sex,

> Yet ne'er so sure our passion to create,
> As when she touch'd the brink of all we hate.

In what light this sally places men and women, I shall leave to the judicious to determine; meanwhile I shall content myself with observing, that I cannot discover why, unless they are mortal, females should always be degraded by being made subservient to love or lust.

To speak disrespectfully of love is, I know, high treason against sentiment and fine feelings; but I wish to speak the simple language of truth, and rather to address the head than the heart. To endeavour to reason love out of the world, would be to out Quixote Cervantes, and equally offend against common sense; but an endeavour to restrain this tumultuous passion, and to prove that it should not be allowed to dethrone superior powers, or to usurp the sceptre which the understanding should ever coolly wield, appears less wild.

Youth is the season for love in both sexes; but in those days of thoughtless enjoyment provision should be made for the more important years of life, when reflection takes place of sensation. But Rousseau, and most of the male writers who have followed his steps, have warmly inculcated that the whole tendency of female education ought to be directed to one point:—to render them pleasing.

Let me reason with the supporters of this opinion who have any knowledge of human nature, do they imagine that marriage can eradicate the habitude of life? The woman who has only been taught to please will soon find that her charms are oblique sunbeams, and that they cannot have much effect on her husband's heart when they are seen every day, when the summer is passed and gone. Will she then have sufficient native energy to look into herself for comfort, and cultivate her dormant faculties? or, is it not more rational to expect that she will try to please other men; and, in the emotions raised by the expectation of new conquests, endeavour to forget the mortification her love or pride has received? When the husband ceases to be a lover—and the time will inevitably come, her desire of pleasing will then grow languid, or become a spring of bitterness; and love, perhaps, the most evanescent of all passions, gives place to jealousy or vanity.

I now speak of women who are restrained by principle or prejudice; such women, though they would shrink from an intrigue with real abhorrence, yet nevertheless, wish to be convinced by the homage of gallantry that they are cruelly neglected by their husbands; or, days and weeks are spent in dreaming of the happiness enjoyed by congenial souls till their health is undermined and their spirits broken by discontent. How then can the great art of pleasing be such a necessary study? it is only useful to a mistress; the chaste wife, and serious mother, should only consider her power to please as the polish of her virtues, and the affection of her husband as one of the comforts that render her task less difficult and her life happier. But, whether she be loved or neglected, her first wish should be to make herself respectable, and not to rely for all her happiness on a being subject to like infirmities with herself.

The worthy Dr. Gregory fell into a similar error. I respect his heart; but entirely disapprove of his celebrated Legacy to his Daughters.

He advises them to cultivate a fondness for dress, because a fondness for dress, he asserts, is natural to them. I am unable to comprehend what either he or Rousseau mean, when they frequently use this indefinite term. If they told us that in a pre-existent state the soul was fond of dress, and brought this inclination with it into a new body, I should listen to them with a half smile, as I often do when I hear a rant about innate elegance. But if he only meant to say that the exercise of the faculties will produce this fondness—I deny it. It is not natural; but arises, like false ambition in men, from a love of power.

Dr. Gregory goes much further; he actually recommends dissimulation, and advises an innocent girl to give the lie to her feelings, and not dance with spirit, when gaiety of heart would make her feet eloquent without making her gestures immodest. In the name of truth and common sense, why should not one woman acknowledge that she can take more exercise than another? or, in other words, that she has a sound constitution; and why, to damp innocent vivacity, is she darkly to be told that men will draw conclusions which she little thinks of?—Let the libertine draw what inference he pleases; but, I hope, that no sensible mother will restrain the natural frankness of youth by instilling such indecent cautions. Out of the abundance of the heart the mouth speaketh; and a wiser than Solomon hath said, that the heart should be made clean, and not trivial ceremonies observed, which it is not very difficult to fulfil with scrupulous exactness when vice reigns in the heart.

Women ought to endeavour to purify their heart; but can they do so when their uncultivated understandings make them entirely dependent on their senses for employment and amusement, when no noble pursuit sets them above the little vanities of the day, or enables them to curb the wild emotions that agitate a reed over which every passing breeze has power? To gain the affections of a virtuous man, is affectation necessary? Nature has given woman a weaker frame than man; but, to ensure her husband's affections, must a wife, who by the exercise of her mind and body whilst she was discharging the duties of a daughter, wife, and mother, has allowed her constitution to retain its natural strength, and her nerves a healthy tone, is she, I say, to condescend to use art and feign a sickly delicacy in order to secure her husband's affection? Weakness may excite tenderness, and gratify the arrogant pride of man; but the lordly caresses of a protector will not gratify a noble mind that pants for, and deserves to be respected. Fondness is a poor substitute for friendship!

In a seraglio, I grant, that all these arts are necessary; the epicure must have his palate tickled, or he will sink into apathy; but have women so little ambition as to be satisfied with such a condition? Can they supinely dream life away in the lap of pleasure, or the languor of weariness, rather than assert their claim to pursue reasonable pleasures and render themselves conspicuous by practising the virtues which dignify mankind? Surely she has not an immortal soul who can loiter life away merely employed to adorn her person, that she may amuse the languid hours, and soften the cares of a fellow-creature who is willing to be enlivened by her smiles and tricks, when the serious business of life is over.

Besides, the woman who strengthens her body and exercises her mind will, by managing her family and practising various virtues, become the friend, and not the humble dependent of her husband; and if she, by possessing such substantial qualities, merit his regard, she will not find it necessary to conceal her affection, nor to pretend to an unnatural coldness of constitution to excite her husband's passions. In fact, if we revert to history, we shall find that the women who have distinguished themselves have neither been the most beautiful nor the most gentle of their sex.

Nature, or, to speak with strict propriety, God, has made all things right; but man has sought him out many inventions to mar the work. I now allude to that part of Dr. Gregory's treatise, where he advises a wife never to let her husband know the extent of her sensibility or affection. Voluptuous precaution, and as ineffectual as absurd. Love, from its very nature, must be transitory. To seek for a secret that would render it constant, would be as wild a search as for the philosopher's stone, or the grand panacea: and the discovery would be equally useless, or rather pernicious, to mankind. The most holy band of society is friendship. It has been well said, by a shrewd satirist, "that rare as true love is, true friendship is still rarer."

This is an obvious truth, and the cause not lying deep, will not elude a slight glance of inquiry.

Love, the common passion, in which chance and sensation take place of choice and reason, is, in some degree, felt by the mass of mankind; for it is not necessary to speak, at present, of the emotions that rise above or sink below love. This passion, naturally increased by suspense and difficulties, draws the mind out of its accustomed state, and exalts the affections; but the security of marriage, allowing the fever of love to subside, a healthy temperature is thought insipid, only by those who have not sufficient intellect to substitute the calm tenderness of friendship, the confidence of respect, instead of blind admiration, and the sensual emotions of fondness.

This is, must be, the course of nature—friendship or indifference inevitably succeeds love. And this constitution seems perfectly to harmonize with the system of government which prevails in the moral world. Passions are spurs to action, and open the mind; but they sink into mere appetites, become a personal and momentary gratification, when the object is gained, and the satisfied mind rests in enjoyment. The man who had some virtue whilst he was struggling for a crown, often becomes a voluptuous tyrant when it graces his brow; and, when the lover is not lost in the husband, the dotard, a prey to childish caprices, and fond jealousies, neglects the serious duties of life, and the caresses which should excite confidence in his children are lavished on the overgrown child, his wife.

In order to fulfil the duties of life, and to be able to pursue with vigour the various employments which form the moral character, a master and mistress of a family ought not to continue to love each other with passion. I mean to say, that they ought not to indulge those emotions which disturb the order of society, and engross the thoughts that should be otherwise employed. The mind that has never been engrossed by one object wants vigour —if it can long be so, it is weak.

A mistaken education, a narrow, uncultivated mind, and many sexual prejudices, tend to make women more constant than men; but, for the present, I shall not touch on this branch of the subject. I will go still further, and advance, without dreaming of a paradox, that an unhappy marriage is often very advantageous to a family, and that the neglected wife is, in general, the best mother. And this would almost always be the consequence if the female mind were more enlarged: for, it seems to be the common dispensation of Providence, that what we gain in present enjoyment should be deducted from the treasure of life, experience; and that when we are gathering the flowers of the day and revelling in pleasure, the solid fruit of toil and wisdom should not be caught at the same time. The way lies before us, we must turn to the right or left; and he who will pass life away in bounding from one pleasure to another, must not complain if he acquire neither wisdom nor respectability of character.

Supposing, for a moment, that the soul is not immortal, and

that man was only created for the present scene,—I think we should have reason to complain that love, infantine fondness, ever grew insipid and palled upon the sense. Let us eat, drink, and love, for to-morrow we die, would be, in fact, the language of reason, the morality of life; and who but a fool would part with a reality for a fleeting shadow? But, if awed by observing the improvable powers of the mind, we disdain to confine our wishes or thoughts to such a comparatively mean field of action; that only appears grand and important, as it is connected with a boundless prospect and sublime hopes, what necessity is there for falsehood in conduct, and why must the sacred majesty of truth be violated to detain a deceitful good that saps the very foundation of virtue? Why must the female mind be tainted by coquettish arts to gratify the sensualist, and prevent love from subsiding into friendship, or compassionate tenderness, when there are not qualities on which friendship can be built? Let the honest heart show itself, and *reason* teach passion to submit to necessity; or, let the dignified pursuit of virtue and knowledge raise the mind above those emotions which rather embitter than sweeten the cup of life, when they are not restrained within due bounds.

I do not mean to allude to the romantic passion, which is the concomitant of genius. Who can clip its wing? But that grand passion not proportioned to the puny enjoyments of life, is only true to the sentiment, and feeds on itself. The passions which have been celebrated for their durability have always been unfortunate. They have acquired strength by absence and constitutional melancholy. The fancy has hovered round a form of beauty dimly seen—but familiarity might have turned admiration into disgust; or, at least, into indifference, and allowed the imagination leisure to start fresh game. With perfect propriety, according to this view of things, does Rousseau make the mistress of his soul, Eloisa, love St. Preux, when life was fading before her; but this is no proof of the immortality of the passion.

Of the same complexion is Dr. Gregory's advice respecting delicacy of sentiment, which he advises a woman not to acquire, if she have determined to marry. This determination, however, perfectly consistent with his former advice, he calls *indelicate*, and earnestly persuades his daughters to conceal it, though it may govern their conduct:—as if it were indelicate to have the common appetites of human nature.

Noble morality! and consistent with the cautious prudence of a little soul that cannot extend its views beyond the present minute division of existence. If all the faculties of woman's mind are only to be cultivated as they respect her dependence on man; if, when a husband be obtained, she have arrived at her goal, and meanly proud rests satisfied with such a paltry crown, let her grovel contentedly, scarcely raised by her employments above the animal kingdom; but, if, struggling for the prize of her high calling, she look beyond the present scene, let her cultivate her understanding without stopping to consider what character the husband may have whom she is destined to marry. Let her only determine, without being too anxious about present happiness, to acquire the qualities that ennoble a rational being, and a rough inelegant husband may shock her taste without destroying her peace of mind. She will not model her soul to suit the frailties of her companion, but to bear with them: his character may be a trial, but not an impediment to virtue.

If Dr. Gregory confined his remark to romantic expectations of constant love and congenial feelings, he should have recollected that experience will banish what advice can never make us cease to wish for, when the imagination is kept alive at the expense of reason.

I own it frequently happens that women who have fostered a romantic unnatural delicacy of feeling, waste their lives in *imagining* how happy they should have been with a husband who could love them with a fervid increasing affection every day, and all day. But they might as well pine married as single—and would not be a jot more unhappy with a bad husband than longing for a good one. That a proper education; or, to speak with more precision, a well stored mind, would enable a woman to support a single life with dignity, I grant; but that she should avoid cultivating her taste, lest her husband should occasionally shock it, is quitting a substance for a shadow. To say the truth, I do not know of what use is an improved taste, if the individual be not rendered more independent of the casualties of life; if new sources of enjoyment, only dependent on the solitary operations of the mind, are not opened. People of taste, married or single, without distinction, will ever be disgusted by various things that touch not less observing minds. On this conclusion the argument must not be allowed to hinge; but in the whole sum of enjoyment is taste to be denominated a blessing?

The question is, whether it procures most pain or pleasure? The answer will decide the propriety of Dr. Gregory's advice, and show how absurd and tyrannic it is thus to lay down a system of slavery; or to attempt to educate moral beings by any other rules than those deduced from pure reason, which apply to the whole species.

Gentleness of manners, forbearance and long-suffering, are such amiable God-like qualities, that in sublime poetic strains the Deity has been invested with them; and, perhaps, no representation of his goodness so strongly fastens on the human affections as those that represent him abundant in mercy and willing to pardon. Gentleness, considered in this point of view, bears on its front all the characteristics of grandeur, combined with the winning graces of condescension; but what a different aspect it assumes when it is the submissive demeanour of dependence, the support of weakness that loves, because it wants protection; and is forbearing, because it must silently endure injuries; smiling under the lash at which it dare not snarl. Abject as this picture appears, it is the portrait of an accomplished woman, according to the received opinion of female excellence, separated by specious reasoners from human excellence. Or, they kindly restore the rib, and make one moral being of a man and woman; not forgetting to give her all the "submissive charms."

How women are to exist in that state where there is to be neither marrying or giving in marriage, we are not told. For though moralists have agreed that the tenor of life seems to prove that *man* is prepared by various circumstances for a future state, they constantly concur in advising *woman* only to provide for the present. Gentleness, docility, and a spaniel-like affection are, on this ground, consistently recommended as the cardinal virtues of the sex; and, disregarding the arbitrary economy of nature, one writer has declared that it is masculine for a woman to be melancholy. She was created to be the toy of man, his rattle, and it must jingle in his ears whenever, dismissing reason, he chooses to be amused.

To recommend gentleness, indeed, on a broad basis is strictly philosophical. A frail being should labour to be gentle. But when forbearance confounds right and wrong, it ceases to be a virtue; and, however convenient it may be found in a companion—that companion will ever be considered as an inferior, and only inspire a vapid tenderness, which easily degenerates into contempt. Still, if advice could really make a being gentle, whose natural disposition admitted not of such a fine polish, something towards the advancement of order would be attained; but if, as might quickly be demonstrated, only affectation be produced by this indiscriminate counsel, which throws a stumbling-block in the way of gradual improvement, and true melioration of temper, the sex is not much benefited by sacrificing solid virtues to the attainment of superficial graces, though for a few years they may procure the individuals regal sway.

As a philosopher, I read with indignation the plausible epithets which men use to soften their insults; and, as a moralist, I ask what is meant by such heterogeneous associations, as fair defects, amiable weaknesses, &c.? If there be but one criterion of morals, but one archetype for man, women appear to be suspended by destiny, according to the vulgar tale of Mahomet's coffin; they have neither the unerring instinct of brutes, nor are allowed to fix the eye of reason on a perfect model. They were made to be loved, and must not aim at respect, lest they should be hunted out of society as masculine.

But to view the subject in another point of view. Do passive indolent women make the best wives? Confining our discussion to the present moment of existence, let us see how such weak creatures perform their part? Do the women who, by the attainment of a few superficial accomplishments, have strengthened the prevailing prejudice, merely contribute to the happiness of their husbands? Do they display their charms merely to amuse them? And have women, who have early imbibed notions of passive obedience, sufficient character to manage a family or educate children? So far from it, that, after surveying the history of woman, I cannot help, agreeing with the severest satirist, considering the sex as the weakest as well as the most oppressed half of the species. What does history disclose but marks of inferiority, and how few women have emancipated themselves from the galling yoke of sovereign man?—So few, that the exceptions remind me of an ingenious conjecture respecting Newton: that he was probably a being of superior order, accidentally caged in a human body. Following the same train of thinking, I have been led to imagine that the few extraordinary women who have rushed in eccentrical directions out of the orbit prescribed to their sex, were *male* spirits, confined by mistake in female frames. But if it be not philosophical to think of sex when the soul is mentioned, the inferiority must depend on the organs; or the heavenly fire, which is to ferment the clay, is not given in equal portions.

But avoiding, as I have hitherto done, any direct comparison of the two sexes collectively, or frankly acknowledging the inferiority of woman, according to the present appearance of things, I shall only insist that men have increased that inferiority till women are almost sunk below the standard of rational creatures. Let their faculties have room to unfold, and their virtues to gain strength, and then determine where the whole sex must stand in the intellectual scale. Yet let it be remembered, that for a small number of distinguished women I do not ask a place.

It is difficult for us purblind mortals to say to what height human discoveries and improvements may arrive when the gloom of despotism subsides, which makes us stumble at every step; but, when morality shall be settled on a more solid basis, then, without being gifted with a prophetic spirit, I will venture to predict that woman will be either the friend or slave of man. We shall not, as at present, doubt whether she is a moral agent, or the link which unites man with brutes. But, should it then appear, that like the brutes they were principally created for the use of man, he will let them patiently bite the bridle, and not mock them with empty praise; or, should their rationality be proved, he will not impede their improvement merely to gratify his sensual appetites. He will not, with all the graces of rhetoric, advise them to submit implicitly their understanding to the guidance of man. He will not, when he treats of the education of women, assert that they ought never to have the free use of reason, nor would he recommend cunning and dissimulation to beings who are acquiring, in like manner as himself, the virtues of humanity.

Surely there can be but one rule of right, if morality has an eternal foundation, and whoever sacrifices virtue, strictly so called, to present convenience, or whose *duty* it is to act in such a manner, lives only for the passing day, and cannot be an accountable creature.

The poet then should have dropped his sneer when he says,

> If weak women go astray,
> The stars are more in fault than they.

For that they are bound by the adamantine chain of destiny is most certain, if it be proved that they are never to exercise their own reason, never to be independent, never to rise above opinion, or to feel the dignity of a rational will that only bows to God, and often forgets that the universe contains any being but itself and the model of perfection to which its ardent gaze is turned, to adore attributes that, softened into virtues, may be imitated in kind, though the degree overwhelms the enraptured mind.

If, I say, for I would not impress by declamation when Reason offers her sober light, if they be really capable of acting like rational creatures, let them not be treated like slaves; or, like the brutes who are dependent on the reason of man, when they associate with him; but cultivate their minds, give them the salutary, sublime curb of principle, and let them attain conscious dignity by feeling themselves only dependent on God. Teach them, in common with man, to submit to necessity, instead of giving, to render them more pleasing, a sex to morals.

Further, should experience prove that they cannot attain the same degree of strength of mind, perseverance, and fortitude, let their virtues be the same in kind, though they may vainly struggle for the same degree; and the superiority of man will be equally clear, if not clearer; and truth, as it is a simple principle, which admits of no modification, would be common to both. Nay, the order of society as it is at present regulated would not be inverted, for woman would then only have the rank that reason assigned her, and arts could not be practised to bring the balance even, much less to turn it.

These may be termed Utopian dreams. Thanks to that Being who impressed them on my soul, and gave me sufficient strength of mind to dare to exert my own reason, till, becoming dependent only on him for the support of my virtue, I view, with indignation, the mistaken notions that enslave my sex.

I love man as my fellow; but his sceptre, real, or usurped, extends not to me, unless the reason of an individual demands my homage; and even then the submission is to reason, and not to man. In fact, the conduct of an accountable being must be regulated by the operations of its own reason; or on what foundation rests the throne of God?

It appears to me necessary to dwell on these obvious truths, because females have been insulated, as it were; and, while they have been stripped of the virtues that should clothe humanity, they have been decked with artificial graces that enable them to exercise a short-lived tyranny. Love, in their bosoms, taking place of every nobler passion, their sole ambition is to be fair, to raise emotion instead of inspiring respect; and this ignoble desire, like the servility in absolute monarchies, destroys all strength of character. Liberty is the mother of virtue, and if women be, by their very constitution, slaves, and not allowed to breathe the sharp invigorating air of freedom, they must ever languish like exotics, and be reckoned beautiful flaws in nature.

As to the argument respecting the subjection in which the sex has ever been held, it retorts on man. The many have always been enthralled by the few; and monsters, who scarcely have shewn any discernment of human excellence, have tyrannized over thousands of their fellow-creatures. Why have men of superior endowments submitted to such degradation? For, is it not universally acknowledged that kings, viewed collectively, have ever been inferior, in abilities and virtue, to the same number of men taken from the common mass of mankind—yet, have they not, and are they not still treated with a degree of reverence that is an insult to reason? China is not the only country where a living man has been made a God. *Men* have submitted to superior strength to enjoy with impunity the pleasure of the moment

—*women* have only done the same, and therefore till it is proved that the courtier, who servilely resigns the birthright of a man, is not a moral agent, it cannot be demonstrated that woman is essentially inferior to man because she has always been subjugated.

Brutal force has hitherto governed the world, and that the science of politics is in its infancy, is evident from philosophers scrupling to give the knowledge most useful to man that determinate distinction.

I shall not pursue this argument any further than to establish an obvious inference, that as sound politics diffuse liberty, mankind, including woman, will become more wise and virtuous.

Notes

DEDICATION

Talleyrand's pamphlet was a *Report on Public Education* (1791), which called for free public education but made no reference to the education of women.

"That to see one half of the human race excluded . . ." seems to be a free translation from Talleyrand's *Report*: "sur quel principe l'un des deux [sexes] pourroit-il en être désherité par la Société protectrice des droits de tous?" This is certainly belied by the French Constitution of 1791, which confined citizenship to males over twenty-five.

CHAPTER II

Wollstonecraft acutely recognizes the disparagement implicit in John Milton's glowing descriptions of Eve. See *Paradise Lost,* IV, 297–99. Her later references are to IV, 634–38, VIII, 381–91, IV, 497–99, X, 891–92 (Cf. Pope, *Moral Essays,* II, 43).

Jean-Jacques Rousseau, a primitivist, believed that civilization corrupted the natural goodness of human nature. Though a strong advocate of liberty, he emphatically did not extend it to women. In *Emile* (1762), he described the ideal education of a boy, in which his natural capacities would be allowed to develop spontaneously. But there is no free development for Emile's female counterpart, Sophie, whose aim in life is simply to please him. Woman was created for man, Rousseau believed; "formed to obey a creature so imperfect as man," she had best learn compliance (Everyman edition, p. 333). Julie and St. Preux are the protagonists of Rousseau's great tragic novel, *Julie: The New Héloise* (1761). Julie is supposed to represent a woman with whom Rousseau was passionately in love.

Dr. John Gregory's *A Father's Legacy to His Daughters* (1774) was widely read and respected for its safely conventional morality and its kindly intentions. The quotations to which Wollstonecraft refers (here taken from the Garland reprint, New York, 1974) are:

> The love of dress is natural to you, and therefore it is proper and reasonable. (*p. 55*)

> I would have you dance with spirit; but never allow yourself to be so far transported with mirth, as to forget the delicacy of your sex.— Many a girl dancing in the gaiety and innocence of her heart, is thought to discover a spirit she little dreams of. (*pp. 57–58*)

> If you are determined at all events to marry, I would advise you to make all your reading and amusements of such a kind as do not affect the heart, nor the imagination, except in the way of wit and humour. (*p. 70*)

Alexander Pope saw woman's charm in her irrationality. See *Moral Essays,* II, 51–52.

"women who have fostered a romantic unnatural delicacy of feeling . . ."—Wollstonecraft noted: "For example, the herd of novelists."

"that state where there is to be neither marrying nor giving in marriage"—eternal life in Heaven, supposedly the goal of all Christians, male and female. See Matthew 22:30.

Bibliographical Note

Wollstonecraft published *Thoughts on the Education of Daughters* (1787), *Mary: A Fiction* (1788), *Original Stories from Real Life* (1788), *A Vindication of the Rights of Men* (1790), *A Vindication of the Rights of Woman* (1792), *An Historical and Moral View of the Origin and Progress of the French Revolution* (1794), *Letters Written During a Short Residence in Sweden, Norway, and Denmark* (1796), and numerous reviews, anthologies, and translations. After her death, Godwin brought out *Posthumous Works of the Author of a Vindication of the*

Rights of Woman (1798), of which the most interesting is the unfinished novel *Maria, or The Wrongs of Woman.*

The best biographies are those of Ralph M. Wardle, *Mary Wollstonecraft: A Critical Biography* (Lawrence: University of Kansas Press, 1951), and Eleanor Flexner, *Mary Wollstonecraft* (New York: Coward, McCann and Geoghegan, 1972). *Shelley and His Circle,* ed. Kenneth Neill Cameron (Cambridge: Harvard University Press, 1961) contains material on Wollstonecraft.